How to Survive Death & Dying

A Guide for Caring for You or Your Loved Ones from Death through Final Disposition

D1377927

by
Gary R. Davis

Mentor Publishing[TM]—*Las Vegas, Nevada*

Mentor Publishing™, 2980 S. Rainbow Blvd., Ste. 116, Las Vegas, NV 89146, (866) 335-4455, FuneralMentor.com.

This book is dedicated to my beloved brother, whose premature death at thirty-seven served to deepen my desire to help people prepare for that inevitable day we all face. C.K. was not only my brother and business partner, he was my best friend. I will miss him always.

CONTENTS

ABOUT THE AUTHOR

Experienced death of a beloved family member

Holds an Associate Degree in Mortuary Science

Licensed funeral director and embalmer for more than 20 years
Owned funeral homes, a crematory, and a cemetery, handling 1,500 deaths a
    year
Owned a preneed sales organization
Coordinated arrangements and conducted funerals for fraternal, ethnic,
    religious, and nondenominational services
Assisted estate-planning attorneys in areas of probate/wills, asset
    preservation, living wills, and trust/estate planning
Licensed insurance agent

State Board of Funeral Directors and Embalmers: Served nine years;
    appointed by two governors
Worked with State Legislature to pass several funeral industry-associated bills
National Funeral Directors' Association Officer
Spoke nationally at State Funeral Director Association conventions

Assisted teaching death and dying courses/classes to college students,
    nurses in training, and hospice volunteers
Worked extensively with families, hospitals, hospice organizations, coroners'
    offices, police departments, the Veterans Administration, Social Security
    Administration, and Bureau of Vital Statistics

Community speaker: elementary and high schools; church, youth, and senior
    groups
Sponsored and coached Little League baseball and basketball teams
Involved in activities to provide recovery for crippled and burned children
Associated with several regional and national charities
Continuing scholarship donor for several colleges

PREFACE

With your acceptance that I am both professionally knowledgeable and compassionate from personal experience, I hope you will allow me to walk with you through necessary information-gathering and decisions to be made when someone dies.

Most of my working life has been spent caring for families seeking assistance when death occurs. I have willingly chosen sleepless nights to try to help grieving loved ones left behind. I have witnessed chaos created when a civic leader, business owner, spouse, parent, child, friend, or associate dies. I surely uttered "I know what you're going through" thousands of times as I tried to console the grief-stricken. But I discovered just how little I really understood, until it happened to me, the day my brother died.

Then I knew. I knew firsthand how painfully and ceaselessly difficult it can be from the moment we are notified a loved one has died through the days that follow. Until I sat on the other side of the funeral director desk, I never fully appreciated how much information has to be known (or quickly researched); how many often-painful decisions must be made; or the level of instantaneous organization and scheduling necessary—added to the weight of indescribable sorrow.

We plan for tornadoes, car wrecks, fires, all forms of disasters, never certain they will ever happen to us; we even carry umbrellas not knowing if it will rain. Yet, few prepare for death, the one and only way to exit life. By not planning for its inevitability, the burden left to others is much greater than need be.

This book was written to help alleviate confusion and, if only to some small measure, grief caused by the death of a loved one. It is meant to clearly prepare you for decisions you must make and information that will be needed either in *(a)* preplanning for your own end, or *(b)* to guide you in the event of the death of a loved one whether foreseen or unexpected.

AFTER-DEATH GUIDELINES
Chapter 1

Over the river they beckon to me,
Loved ones who've crossed to the farther side,
The gleam of their snowy robes I see,
    But their voices are lost in the dashing tide.
There's one with ringlets of sunny gold,
    And eyes the reflection of heaven's own blue;
He crossed in the twilight gray and cold,
    And the pale mist hid him from mortal view.
We saw not the angels who met him there,
    The gates of the city we could not see:
Over the river, over the river,
    My brother stands waiting to welcome me.

Nancy Amelia Woodbury Priest

FIRST NOTIFICATION OF DEATH

Depending on where a death occurs and what circumstances surround it dictates how and when the next of kin is/are notified.

Hospital, Convalescent Center, Hospice Facility
These are today's prevailing locations for death. More often than not a family member is present; so it is not always a shock when a family is told by a nurse or physician that death has occurred.

Home
When death occurs at home, it is usually unexpected. There are, of course, instances of imminent or expected death when the decision to die at home has been made by the individual or the family. In either event, someone present should notify medical emergency personnel (911), a home care nurse, or the attending physician.

Physician vs Coroner
City, county, or state governments dictate whether the attending physician or the coroner (commonly a pathologist in larger metropolitan areas, but not always required) will determine the death and subsequently sign the death certificate.

The general rule is that a physician can pronounce the death and sign the death certificate if: *(a)* (s)he is present at the patient's death; *(b)* if the patient has been in a hospital for a specified number of hours—generally 24 or 48; and/or *(c)* if the patient has been under the care of a physician who determines sufficient reason to certify the cause of death.

The coroner will pronounce the death and sign the death certificate if: (a) there is no attending physician; (b) the physician does not have sufficient reason to certify as to the cause of death. It is also necessary for the coroner to be involved if the death is due to any perceived form of trauma (including violence or crime), regardless of where death occurs. It is important to note that a coroner, an extension of the local police department, becomes involved in a death suspected of anything other than natural causes.

Notification
In all situations, it is the duty of the physician, coroner, or their appointed representative, to notify the legal next of kin (or his/her designated representative) of the death, and to attest as to the cause of death on the death certificate.

Death Certificate
Hospitals, by law, prepare a birth certificate when a baby is born. The hospital, physician, and/or coroner are obliged to provide correct information and signatures following a death, so that the funeral director can properly complete and file the death certificate. A death certificate is a legal document which must *(a)* contain correct statistical information, *(b)* be signed by the attending physician or coroner, and *(c)* be filed with the county or state health department. The death certificate must list the cause of death and be accepted by the health registrar before a burial, cremation, or any other final disposition can take place.

If the next of kin is unprepared or does not know answers to the questions, it can turn into a tedious task to provide the required statistical data for the funeral director/adviser. It is recommended, therefore, that the historical information (see *Information Needed to Complete Certificate of Death* Form in Chapter 12) be researched and listed to more easily process correct answers and ensure that this vital information is submitted to the adviser error-free. Even the slightest mistake can be costly, can slow down the process of disposition, and consequently, delay the receipt of available benefits.

One (1) original death certificate is completed, recorded with the county or state. "Certified" copies can then be purchased. A certified copy is necessary for many reasons, such as applying for union, pension, or Social Security benefits; life insurance proceeds; property transfers; and completion of estate work. Each state sets its fees for certified copies of the death certificate. (A <u>sample</u> *Certificate of Death* is included in Chapter 12.)

IMMEDIATE DECISIONS

Once the notification has been made to next of kin, there are decisions that must be made within minutes, and several others soon afterward. The burden of making decisions is multiplied when the death is unexpected. This is especially true if no previous preparation, planning, or even conscious thought was given to the possibility of death. Following are the most common *immediate* decisions to be made.

Organ Donation

Not everyone can be an organ donor. Nevertheless, it is important to inform your family or legal representative if you wish to donate your organs in the event of your death. Most donors are recognized by the phrase "Organ Donor," appearing on a driver's license or identification card. The decision to accept the organ(s) or tissue rests with the organ donor bank contacted either prior to a pending death or at the time of an unexpected death. The most common reasons a decedent does not become an organ donor are: *(a)* if his or her wishes are unknown; *(b)* a time lapse between time of death and discovery; *(c)* if organs were damaged due to the cause of death; or *(d)* because of medications used to attempt to keep the patient alive.

Once again, if the coroner is in charge of the death certification, (s)he decides on any donation. The request to donate organs may also be denied if such donation might hamper the investigation as to the exact cause of death.

Autopsy

An autopsy is a surgical procedure to examine internal body organs to more conclusively determine cause of death. In plain terms, this means that all internal body organs will be removed and examined with a small portion of each dissected organ retained for microscopic study by the pathologist. If a coroner is involved at the time of death, (s)he decides if an autopsy will be performed. If a coroner is not involved, an autopsy becomes the option of the next of kin. However, under no circumstances can a coroner's decision to perform an autopsy be overridden.

Very often, the attending physician or hospital requests permission to perform an autopsy. The next of kin is free to grant or deny such request. Under these circumstances, it is performed at no charge to the next of kin. However, if the family chooses an autopsy, it is likely to be at their expense. An autopsy rarely causes delays in planning for a funeral date. (*Authorization for Autopsy* form is included in Chapter 12.)

Funeral Home Selection

No matter where death occurs, one of the first questions the next of kin is asked upon notification of death is, "Which funeral home would you like us to contact to remove the body?" It is imperative that family members are made aware of prearranged plans with a funeral home so that the wishes of the deceased are fulfilled. It is also important to know this information because, very often, the arrangements are already paid for.

In most cases, if next of kin (or designated representative) does not immediately choose the funeral home, the hospital or coroner makes the selection—based on some form of contract removal or a rotation basis with local funeral homes. One of the first documents the next of kin may be required to sign is a release form directing the hospital/coroner to contact a specific funeral home. As soon as the funeral home is notified of the death and release, a vehicle is dispatched to remove the deceased. (*Authorization for Release of Remains* form may be found in Chapter 12.)

Arrangement Time

The funeral home will ask the next of kin (or representative) for a meeting with them to complete the service arrangements. An *arrangement conference* at the funeral home will last one to one and one-half (1-1 1/2) hours. The time may be shortened if the next of kin (representative) possesses the proper information, particularly if any prearrangements were made. The decision-makers should all be present at the *arrangement conference* if they expect the funeral home to complete the planning in a timely and efficient manner.

Delay Between Death and Service

The most common mistake families make is confirming a funeral/memorial service time prior to meeting with the funeral director. Although every effort is made to accommodate a family's wishes, funeral home calendars must be considered prior to setting days and times for services—to avoid scheduling conflicts. Sufficient time for family members and friends to arrange transportation to the service's city must also be considered if they are away at the time of death or live elsewhere.

Embalming

Embalming is a temporary preservation procedure done to ensure that the decedent is properly disinfected and prepared for the services, if any. The primary reason for embalming is to allow for the most optimum condition of the decedent to be seen at a private or public viewing.

The Federal Trade Commission passed certain rules several years ago specifically addressing what a funeral home can or cannot require a family to do about embalming. There are a few instances in which an embalment is obligatory—such as transportation across state lines or on a common carrier if death occurs away from the city or state of final disposition (burial, entombment, or cremation). However, instead of embalming, should the next of kin choose, *in some instances* the deceased will be placed in a sealed container for transport.

Although the law may not specifically require embalmment, it would be highly unusual for a funeral home to allow the deceased to be publicly viewed without first being embalmed. Such policy is solely at the option of the funeral home.

The Federal Trade Commission requires that the funeral director obtain permission from the next of kin to embalm in order to charge for it. For best results, embalming should proceed as soon as possible after the death. (An *Authorization to Embalm* form is included in Chapter 12.)

LEGAL CONSIDERATIONS
Chapter 2

NEXT OF KIN

Each state has its own laws which specify *(a)* who may qualify as next of kin, and *(b)* in what order of authority the surviving next of kin is recognized.

Responsibility for the financial arrangements does *not* change the authority of the next of kin. That means that even if only some family members accept financial responsibility, decisions to be made regarding the remains' burial, cremation, and/or final disposition are equal among all of the legally accepted next of kin.

It should be noted, however, that many states recognize a prepaid contract and/or legally compiled and filed instructions for burial, cremation, or final disposition if the deceased made his/her own arrangements while living.

Following are the most accepted next-of-kin lines:

1. Spouse

If there is a surviving spouse, then (s)he is likely to be considered the legal next of kin and, therefore, generally has the authority to make all of these decisions. Even if there are adult children from a present or previous marriage, the *current spouse retains the authority* to choose all final disposition arrangements.

2. Surviving Adult Children

Should there be no surviving spouse, many states have established laws to allow surviving adult children to make the necessary decisions, collectively. No one child has more or less authority than another surviving adult child; *however, the majority in agreement* can control the arrangements.

3. Surviving Parents

Legal parents of underage or incapacitated single children usually hold primary authority, as well as being most often considered next of kin in the chain hereto. Surviving parents maintain joint authority, *currently married or not*; or, the surviving parent prevails.

4. Surviving Brothers and Sisters

As in the case of surviving adult children, it is usually the majority of the surviving brothers and sisters who may make decisions.

5. Decedent's Guardian or Personal Representative

If no next of kin is known, or if a guardian or personal representative has been named—in a will or as the result of other legalities or document(s)—that person will take responsibility for carrying out the decedent's wishes, if known. Note that whether a legal representative is appointed by the decedent or the survivor(s), *no financial responsibility is placed upon such representative.*

Once the legal next of kin is established, it is up to him/her/them to decide where the deceased will be taken, if there will be services and disposition, or final disposition only. This includes not only the manner of burial, cremation, and so forth, but whether to move the decedent to another jurisdictional (geographical) location.

If the decedent created a properly drafted will or trust, or other legally filed document(s), designating another person, not next of kin, to act as his/her representative, affording that person (or it may be persons) all rights to arranging final disposition, most jurisdictions will validate that representative as the decedent's legal choice. However, if next of kin opposes such recognition, a court order may be required.

FINANCIAL LIABILITY

As previously stated, there is a vast difference between being next of kin and accepting financial liability. Little can be done to force next of kin to accept financial responsibility upon the death of a family member. If a relative/family chooses not to be involved in any of the arrangements, the funeral home (which was called or assigned to accept the remains) will file for an abandonment with the appropriate city, county, or state, so as to dispose of the decedent. Should the next of kin reject financial responsibility, they are *generally* precluded from selecting any of the service or disposition arrangements.

However, if an agreed upon contract is signed by the next of kin, the funeral home or cemetery has the legal right to enforce payment for services rendered.

ASSETS

Each state has its own specific laws dealing with community and separate assets owned by a married couple.

Most people believe that joint bank accounts and assets should be removed prior to an official notification that a death has occurred. In most instances, due to community property laws or joint accounts, the bank/financial institution treats bank accounts no different because of the death of a depositor.

In actuality, if there is more than one signature recognized as *authorized* to transfer funds (checks or cash), it is likely considered a joint account with equal access and ownership.

It is very important to know and understand the laws of the state where assets are held in order to avoid any confusion at the time of a death. Banks will fully apprise its current and potential customers of their own policies and state banking laws regarding this subject.

POWER OF ATTORNEY

A "Power of Attorney" is a properly executed legal document allowing a second person to sign his/her name *with the same power and authority* as the one who granted the right.

Granting such authority can be both advantageous and a disadvantage for different reasons. It is a *power that* must be carefully considered due to the possibility of misuse. Keeping in mind that the person can legally sign anything you can—*in your name, without your presence or permission*—an exceptional level of trust for that person must be felt, perhaps even verified. Also note that it is not too unusual for an attorney to be given this authority.

Because of illness or aging, many people grant power of attorney to their children, siblings, or close friends, so as to give them the ability to assist in daily activities, which may include banking or transfer of property, only two of many legal transactions requiring mobility and/or complete understanding.

It is *mistakenly* believed, however, that a power of attorney can be used after the person who granted such authority dies. To the contrary, all *power of attorney privileges automatically end upon death of the grantor.*

A <u>sample</u> *General Power of Attorney* follows.

GENERAL POWER OF ATTORNEY

KNOW ALL PERSONS BY THESE PRESENTS: That I, _____,
Grantor's Name

the undersigned, do hereby make, constitute, and appoint _____,
Appointee's Name

as my true and lawful Attorney, in accordance with the Powers of Attorney Act, and to do on my behalf anything that I can lawfully have done by an Attorney.

In accordance with the Powers of Attorney Act, I hereby declare that this Power of Attorney may be exercised during any subsequent legal incapacity on my part.

This Power of Attorney is subject to the following conditions:

_____

_____

_____

IN WITNESS WHEREOF, I have hereunto set my hand this _____ day of

_____,20_____.

_____
Grantor's Signature

_____
Print or Type Name

State of   )
)
County of   )

This instrument was acknowledged before me on this _____ day of _____ , 20_____.

By Notary Public _____

My Commission Expires:_____

MUNICIPAL, STATE, OR NATIONAL LAWS

Laws differ among municipalities or states; national laws govern the entire country.

While specific laws may vary in each of these different jurisdictions, the higher authority *always* takes precedence. For example, if a national law is enacted, it is impossible to change that law at a municipal or state level. State law overrides any county or city ordinance or statute.

Although laws governing the operation of funeral homes, cemeteries, and crematories may vary slightly, national and state laws have become more uniform in recent years. Each state has a regulatory board either elected or, more commonly, appointed to hear complaints from consumers, to ensure that funeral homes, cemeteries, and crematories operate in compliance with applicable laws, and to ascertain that consumers are being treated fairly.

These regulatory boards typically include licensed industry practitioners and consumers to promote fairness to both entities.

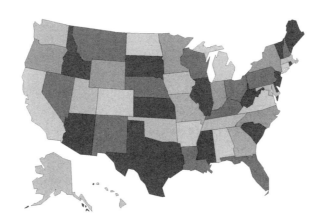

PUBLIC ADMINISTRATOR

A city, county, or state Public Administrator is given the responsibility to secure the assets of the decedent in behalf of the legal next of kin. This office is very important, in that, many people die at home with no relative(s) present. The Public Administrator physically secures the residence and property until next of kin can be notified and the premises released to them.

If there is no known next of kin, the assets are dispersed by this Public Administrator in accordance with provisions of the will—if one exists.

If there is no will, or the will is not specific as to disbursement, the assets will be dispersed in accordance with the intestate laws of the particular state where such assets are located.

As a result of so many unmarried couples now living together, there is often considerable confusion. This is particularly true when a survivor-companion is not listed as the property co-owner or contractual party in a lease, wherever the deceased resides at the time of death. Controversy often arises when adult children from a previous marriage or relationship come forward and are given both legal access to the personal residence and all physical assets secured by the Public Administrator.

This is only one of many good reasons to legally determine any joint ownership which could be questioned, and to maintain a current will that clearly spells out what is to be done concerning the disposition of assets in the event of a death.

Still another reason is that not all cities, counties, or states establish/retain a position such as Public Administrator.

CREMATION

Because cremation is an irreversible process, a crematory must ensure that all legal documents under its particular state's laws are signed by the legal and proper next of kin (or representative in applicable cases).

It does not matter if *legally designated* next-of-kin relatives live in different cities, states, even countries; *each and all* must sign to have cremation authorized.

If it is impossible to acquire all signatures, *some* jurisdictions/states allow cremation to go forward if due diligence has been performed, that is, exhaustive legal attempts made to obtain all of the necessary signatures. One example would be if a brother or sister, estranged from other brothers and sisters, cannot be located. The known surviving brothers and sisters, in this instance, could sign an indemnification agreement allowing the cremation to take place, but only if the jurisdiction's laws agree.

The general rule is that a crematory will not go forward until they are completely satisfied that they have the necessary signature(s) from the next of kin to authorize the cremation. This is readily understandable since a burial allows changes or revisions at any later time; cremation is final.

POLICIES OF FUNERAL HOMES, CEMETERIES, OR CREMATORIES

Although there may not be a specific statute governing each particular practice, it has not been unusual for funeral homes, cemeteries, and crematories to create their own policies; sometimes collectively deemed acceptable, often commonly or regionally followed within the industry.

It is clear that a funeral home cannot require that a body be embalmed in order for a funeral service with the deceased present, except in certain instances. One example is that a funeral home is well within its rights to enforce its own internal policy that no unembalmed remains *may be viewed by the public within the funeral home.*

A cemetery may have a policy which allows them to remove flowers placed on graves to enable them to mow the lawns at any time, even though no established law exists.

Such policies may be enforced as long as they do not violate municipal, state, or national laws.

PRICING

In 1984, the Federal Trade Commission set specific requirements in its "Funeral Service Rule" directing that providers itemize all charges for goods and services they offer to the public. The form containing this information is entitled the "General Price List." (A sample *General Price List* may be found in Chapter 11.)

Although these General Price Lists may somewhat vary in format and/or regional cost-of-living price levels, the Rule requires certain form standardizations so as to provide an exact itemization for the goods and services to the consumer, expressly for price comparison.

The Rule mandates that a General Price List be shown to (and a copy subsequently given to) the consumer before any discussion of funeral goods and services can proceed.

The Funeral Service Rule also states that any person may ask for a copy of the General Price List simply for reference with no current need, which the provider of funeral goods and services must provide.

This law does *not* include cemeteries; however, most cemeteries do offer such an itemized breakdown of their products and services.

FUNERAL AND MEMORIAL SERVICES PLANNING
Chapter 3

SERVICE DECISIONS

It is important to understand that if there is to be a funeral, memorial service, or final disposition without a formal service, a funeral home is, nevertheless, always involved. To clearly relate to you all of the information needed at the time of a death, the basis chosen for this subject is that a service will be held—urging the reader to keep in mind that a service is only one of several options. This will provide a specific explanation of information needed, and potential decisions to be discussed with a funeral director/adviser during a funeral arrangement conference.

Most of the decisions must be made rather quickly. Once all arrangements are confirmed, the funeral home staff has a relatively short time to implement the necessary tasks to ensure that the desires of the family are satisfactorily met.

Funeral or Memorial Service Arrangements

As previously stated, it is important that no services be presumed scheduled and announced prior to meeting with the funeral home and/or church representative to ensure the requested day and time are mutually available. Many elements go into the planning of a funeral or memorial service. The following items show the detail and thought which go into planning a meaningful service for family and friends.

Traditional vs Memorial

The word *traditional*, when referring to funerals, usually means a service with the casket present. The casket may be open or closed, the service may or may not be held at the funeral home, but the casketed deceased is present during the service. Although memorial services are now more commonplace, there will always be families who choose the traditional service.

The *memorial* service focuses on the life of the loved one rather than on the presence of a casket holding the deceased's physical remains. Photo, video, or slide presentations are often presented; sometimes memorabilia special to the deceased such as a saddle, a badge or helmet, artwork, needlework, etc., are displayed. Floral arrangements are usually placed where a casket would have stood.

The best advice for families deciding on which type of service is best for them is to choose the one most meaningful to them. There are no right or wrong answers to this question. Simply taking the time to express to a spouse or children what we, ourselves, would prefer in the event of our own deaths greatly assists family members to more easily choose.

Funeral Home vs Church or Community Center

The best advice for this question depends on several factors. Was the deceased a member of a local church, synagogue, or mosque? Does the place of worship allow services with a casket present? Can it accommodate the number of attending family and friends anticipated?

In some geographic areas and communities, services are expected to be held in places of worship. In fast-growing areas where there is a movement away from some of the more established customs, services are often held at the funeral home or in a community center. Funeral homes with attached facilities can usually accommodate a relatively large number of people. Careful consideration should be given to the anticipated number of attendees to make the decision easier as to where the service should be held.

There is a growing trend to place funeral homes within or adjacent to cemeteries, enabling attendees to walk or drive a short distance for the committal (final burial, entombment, or inurnment) service. In larger communities, traffic might pose a problem, making it more convenient to hold all of the services at one location.

Visitation

Visitation has a set time, generally one or two days prior to the funeral service for friends to gather to pay their respects to the deceased and offer support to the family. When a visitation is held, the casket is present (and may be open or closed).

Volumes have been written, and there will always be debates within families, regarding an open or closed casket. This issue can easily be resolved by *(a)* establishing a brief period to view the deceased by the family, then closing the casket for public visitation; or *(b)* opening the casket for visitation, but closing it during services.

Visitation customs sometimes depend on the geographic area, from as little as a few minutes prior to the service to several days. Religious beliefs must also be considered when discussing visitation. Although it may not be required to embalm in order to hold visitation with an open casket, the vast majority of funeral homes require that the deceased be embalmed if public viewing is intended.

Clergy or Service Coordinator

> *Give sorrow words; the grief that does not speak*
> *Whispers the o'er-fraught heart and bids it break.*
> Shakespeare: Macbeth

The most logical person to conduct the funeral or memorial service is one who shares a religious tie to either the decedent or the family. It is not uncommon, however, for more than one person to conduct the service—sometimes for families sharing different religious affiliations. It is also customary for fraternal organizations to participate in otherwise religious or secular services.

If there are to be no religious or fraternal services, but the participants are family members, friends, and/or community leaders, delegating a person to announce what will take place and introduce those who will speak is recommended. This role should be offered to someone who is comfortable speaking before a gathering, and who can assist in the flow of the service requested by the next of kin.

Music

There is nothing so loud as silence during a time of grief and sadness. Music tends to console people as they enter and exit a service. It also serves to soften the transition between speakers. And when appropriate, nothing reflects someone better than music loved or appreciated during life. Funeral homes, places of worship, and community centers are generally equipped to offer many forms of recorded music. Live musical performance, if tasteful, can add greatly to a service.

It is important that the funeral director, the person officiating the service, and those providing the music, coordinate well in advance to avoid awkwardness or disruption during the service due to lack of planning.

Family Vehicles

Where the service is to be held and whether there will be a procession to the place of interment may dictate the need for family cars. Such decisions would also be based on the emotional state of family members. In today's fast-paced society, traffic can add to stress, and so, to grief. It is better to use professional drivers, ensuring arrival at the service with less difficulty. Transportation is also often provided for officiating clergy and pallbearers from the service to the interment location. If family or friends are coming from other geographic areas, next of kin may choose to provide their transportation on the day of the service.

Procession Escorts

If there is to be a formal procession to the interment site, escorts are highly recommended. Generally, motorcycle escorts are used, most often provided contractually from a private company. Local laws dictate whether a funeral procession is allowed and if escorts are required. Some cities do not have available escorts, or the traffic makes it unfeasible to allow a procession. In such instances, the officiator or funeral director should announce that those traveling to the interment should obey traffic laws, and that sufficient time will be allowed for everyone to gather for the committal portion of the service.

Printed Materials

The most frequently printed materials when there is to be a formal service are a memorial register book and some form of memorial folder. For several religious services a prayer card is also important. With the availability of computer-generated printed materials and high-speed printers, it is possible for funeral homes to provide a greater selection of verses, poetry, and printed materials than ever before. Professional printers also provide many more options, all in time for scheduled services. Several ideas and selections can be found in *Funeral and Memorial Service Ideas*, Chapter 4.

Pallbearers

This area can cause confusion to those asked to serve either as pallbearers or "honorary pallbearers." The usual number of pallbearers is six. While acceptable, using eight pallbearers makes it difficult to move a casket as needed. Selection is often difficult. Historically, pallbearers were close friends, co-workers, and/or business associates, with women rarely included. Today, it is well accepted for family members to serve as pallbearers, including women and children.

Caskets can be heavy, but seldom is one moved without a rolling cart under it. The pallbearers traditionally walk along with the casket guided by the funeral director, with little manual burden placed on them.

Honorary Pallbearers

If also using honorary pallbearers is determined, what is expected of them, if anything, should be made clear. This role ranges from having his/her name printed on the service folder, to walking behind the casket, to simply sitting in a special section during the service. Examples for naming honorary pallbearers can be: *(a)* due to the health consideration of someone, nevertheless, signifying his/her importance to the deceased and the family; and *(b)* too many family members or close friends to limit selection to only six or eight.

Floral Arrangements

Either the funeral adviser or florist can assist in selecting floral arrangements for a funeral or memorial service. If the casket is to be at a service, the first floral piece often selected is a casket spray. If an American flag is to cover the casket to denote military service, however, a floral spray cannot be placed on the casket. A standing floral arrangement in a basket is the better choice in this .case. The florist or funeral home will provide the necessary equipment to display selected flower arrangements.

Many florists include a card to identify the sender, often with a short message of sympathy to the bereaved. Further, funeral homes generally provide a duplicate card to the family at the conclusion of the services so that they have a record of the flowers received, and from whom.

If, in lieu of flowers, the next of kin encourages donations to a particular charity or benefactor, it is important to inform the funeral adviser during the initial conference. Such request may also be included in the obituary. Still considered the universal expression of sympathy, flowers are often sent irrespective of the family's requests.

Military Honors

Families are occasionally disappointed in military honors—not in those given by active military personnel, but by the difficulty in arranging them as part of a funeral or memorial service. How close a military unit is stationed to the funeral or memorial site dictates what can be arranged to honor the decedent who served in the armed forces. Generally, the military guard is in the same service branch as the decedent, i.e., the U.S. Army, Navy, Marines, Air Force, or Coast Guard. Possible military honors include a color guard, an honor guard, or a limited version of one of these special presentations. (See Chapter 6, where *American Veterans' Privileges* are more fully presented.)

Clothing, Cosmetics, Hair

There is no set rule regarding the clothes a person should be buried in. Families are encouraged to select clothes representative of how the decedent most often appeared in public. If, for example, the decedent did not own a suit, it would not be inappropriate to be buried in something other than a suit. It is helpful to bring the clothing to the funeral home for the arrangement conference. Included with outer clothing should be undergarments and socks for men, and undergarments and nylons or socks for women. It is always preferred to select clothing with long sleeves and a high neckline.

A photo of the decedent is also helpful so as to have cosmetics and hair done as close as possible to the decedent's usual life appearance. If (s)he is willing, the decedent's regular hairdresser can come to the funeral home to arrange the decedent's hair.

Jewelry

Most families agree that any jewelry worn by the decedent for visitation or the funeral service should be returned to the next of kin (representative) prior to burial or final disposition. Wedding bands are often buried with the decedent, but it is rare to include additional jewelry. Funeral directors generally discourage bringing expensive jewelry to the funeral home because of the potential liability existing if misplaced or stolen.

It is common practice to prepare an inventory of the jewelry given to the funeral adviser, and to require the next of kin to sign a release of liability for the loss or theft of such jewelry. It is better to bring only items to be included in the final disposition. (A <u>sample</u> *Personal Property Release & Indemnity* form is included in Chapter 12.)

Obituary Notice

The funeral director will contact local newspapers regarding each death for a possible obituary to be published, regardless of type of service and disposition. Printing the information is solely at the option of the newspaper's publisher.

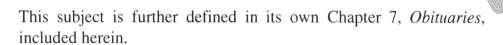

This subject is further defined in its own Chapter 7, *Obituaries*, included herein.

Casket Selection

For those making funeral arrangements for a loved one, the casket selection is often the most difficult part of the arrangement process. This is the best-defined sign that death has really occurred, and that the future will be different for the family.

The "selection room" can consist of as many as twenty or more choices at varying costs. Prices are based on materials used in the construction, interior design, and other features. The Federal Trade Commission imposed rules upon providers of funeral goods and services several years ago which require a complete itemization of the costs associated with these arrangements. It was common practice to use "unit" prices in the past—the casket and funeral services were combined. Today, all available casket prices must be specifically listed. This was done to make the consumer more aware of the price of each casket offered, along with a description of the materials used in construction. (A complete section on caskets is included in Chapter 10.)

CREMATION

A growing number of individuals and families are selecting cremation as the means of final disposition. Many options are available to those choosing cremation who still wish to hold some form of service.

Funeral Service
A complete funeral service can be held prior to the cremation, which may include visitation and services at a funeral home, church, or community center. At its conclusion, the casketed remains are taken to the crematory. The casket may be cremated with the decedent; however, some funeral homes provide a rental casket for the service—an outer shell (casket) with a cremation container inside. Following the service, the container is removed to be used for cremating the decedent.

Memorial Service
A memorial service is an option if there is to be no visitation nor the decedent present for a service. In this case, the cremation may take place as soon as the permits are secured, whether before or after the memorial service.

Possible memorial service locations are endless, but most families tend to agree the service is more meaningful if held at a funeral home, church, or community center. The funeral director's assistance is available just as for any service, as well as the preparation of printed materials.

Direct Cremation
This means that the funeral home will gather the necessary information, secure the cremation permits, and cremate the remains as soon as possible—without a funeral or memorial service.

There are several theories on the value of a funeral or memorial service relating to the grief process within a surviving family. While there is no one answer, it is widely accepted that a service celebrates the life that was lived, bringing friends and family together to express their feelings, and to provide support for one another.

BILLING AND PAYMENT

All funeral homes are required by federal law to supply consumers with a *General Price List* (see sample in Chapter 11) prior to making any funeral service arrangements. This requirement was created to provide consumers with a complete, itemized listing of service and merchandise items offered by funeral homes, including specific charges. This is a standardized form, making it easier for price comparison when selecting among different funeral homes. A General Price List can be obtained by requesting it from a funeral home.

Once all of the arrangements are complete, a funeral home contract—itemizing the charges for all of the funeral goods and services selected that next of kin has agreed to and will be responsible for—is signed.

Method of payment generally includes cash, check, credit card, or a verifiable insurance assignment. Another acceptable method of payment may be a union death benefit or a benefit provided by an industrial insurance policy in the event of an accident-related death.

Rarely will a funeral home accept promised payment from estates or probate, or a payment plan over time. If the next of kin is unable to pay for the services or cannot arrange financing, there are government agencies that assist in such instances.

Information about government aid is further addressed in Chapter 9, *Some Available Benefits*.

FUNERAL AND MEMORIAL SERVICE IDEAS
Chapter 4

Show me the manner in which a nation cares for its dead, and I will measure with mathematical exactness the tender mercies of its people, their respect for the laws of the land and their loyalty to high ideals.

William E. Gladstone

SERVICE IDEAS

Following are a few suggestions which may have meaning for and offer solace to both the family and friends of the decedent.

Pictures or Videos

If the next of kin rejects a public viewing, or an open casket is impossible due to prolonged illness or traumatic death, photographs provide a fitting memorialization of the deceased. Photos may be displayed next to the casket; in lieu of a casket, where—or next to where—it may have been placed; or near the memorial register book. Photos which portray the interest of the deceased or meaningful family group photos are encouraged.

A video or slide presentation with background music may also offer some comfort. It is a way to share what was important to the deceased with family and friends, and often says more than spoken words.

Religious vs Secular Services

If the decedent was a member of a religious faith, it is suggested that a cleric or religious leader of that denomination conduct the service at their place of worship. If, on the other hand, the decedent did not participate in any organized religion, the ceremony should not be based entirely, if at all, upon scripture or theology.

Verses and Poetry

Following are only a few suggestions of verses and poetry common to or befitting a funeral or memorial service. They may be spoken; printed in memorial folders; used in correspondence for notification to friends; or included in an obituary published in newspapers, journals, or newsletters.

Behold...
The
Lord.

THE TWENTY-THIRD PSALM (1)

The Lord is my shepherd; I shall not want.
He maketh me to lie down in green pastures;
He leadeth me beside the still waters.
    He restoreth my soul;
He leadeth me in the paths of righteousness
    for His name's sake.
Yea, though I walk through the valley of the
    shadow of death, I will fear no evil;
    For thou art with me;
Thy rod and Thy staff they comfort me.
Thou preparest a table before me in the
    presence of mine enemies;
Thou anointest my head with oil;
    my cup runneth over.
Surely goodness and mercy shall follow me
    all the days of my life;
And I will dwell in the house of the Lord
    forever. Amen.

THE LORD'S PRAYER (2)

Our Father, who art in heaven,
hallowed be thy name.
Thy kingdom come,
Thy will be done on earth as it is in heaven.
Give us this day our daily bread.
And forgive us our trespasses,
as we forgive those who trespass against us.
And lead us not into temptation,
but deliver us from evil.
For thine is the kingdom, and the power,
and the glory forever. Amen.

PRAYER OF ST. FRANCIS OF ASSISI (3)

Lord, make me an instrument of your peace;
Where there is hatred, let me sow love;
Where there is injury, pardon;
Where there is doubt, faith;
Where there is despair, hope;
Where there is darkness, light;
And where there is sadness, joy.

O Divine Master
Grant that I may not so much
seek to be consoled as to console;
To be understood as to understand;
To be loved as to love.
For it is in giving that we receive;
It is in pardoning that we are pardoned;
And it is in dying that we are
born to eternal life.   Amen.

GOD NEEDED AN ANGEL IN HEAVEN (4)

When Jesus lived upon the earth
    so many years ago,
He called the children close to Him
    because he loved them so...
And with that tenderness of old,
    that same sweet, gentle way,
He holds your little loved one close
    within His arms today...
And you'll find comfort in your faith
    that in His home above
The God of little children
    gives your little one His love...
So think of your little darling
    lighthearted and happy and free
Playing in God's Promised Land
    where there is joy eternally.
                    Author Unknown

FOOTPRINTS (5)

One night a man had a dream. He dreamed he was walking along the beach with the Lord. Across the sky flashed scenes from his life. For each scene, he noticed two sets of footprints in the sand; one belonged to him and the other, the Lord.

When the last scene of his life flashed before him, he looked back at the footprints in the sand. He noticed that many times along the path of his life, there was only one set of footprints. He also noticed that it happened at the very lowest and saddest times in his life.

This really bothered him and he questioned the Lord about it. "Lord, you said that once I decided to follow you, you'd walk with me all the way. But I have noticed that during the most troublesome times in my life, there is only one set of footprints. I don't understand why when I needed you most, you would leave me."

The Lord replied, "My precious, precious child. I love you and I would never leave you. During your times of trial and suffering, when you see only one set of footprints, it was then that I carried you."

Anonymous

SERENITY PRAYER (6)

God grant me the serenity
to accept the things I cannot change,
the courage to change the things I can,
and the wisdom to know the difference.

Reinhold Niebuhr

AN EMPTY CHAIR (7)

There's an empty chair across from me.
There's an empty chair where you used to be.
There's a hum of voices near
    as I eat alone without you dear.
I play the games as we used to do.
But it's not the same, Dear Heart, without you.
When you passed away I must confess,
    I lost my love and all my happiness.
The morning sun brings no relief
    from the dark night of total grief.
Why must I live? While you are gone?
Without you love, I don't belong.
There's an empty chair across from me.
Dear Lord let me join you for all eternity.
Then there'll be no empty chair across from me.
There'll be two empty chairs,
    One for you, and one for me.

                     Keotah M. Fannin

SAFELY HOME (8)

I am home in heaven, dear ones.
Oh, so happy and so bright!
There is a perfect joy and beauty
In the everlasting light.
All the pain and grief is over,
Every restless tossing passed;
I am now at peace forever,
Safely home in heaven at last.

There is work still waiting for you,
So you must not idly stand.
Do it now, while life remaineth-
You shall rest in God's own land.
When that work is all completed,
He will gently call you home.
Oh, the rapture of that meeting;
Oh, the joy to see you come!

                     Author Unknown

MISS ME - BUT LET ME GO (9)

When I come to the end of the road
    And the sun has set on me,
I want no rites in a gloom–filled room,
    Why cry for a soul set free?
Miss me a little–but not too long,
    And not with your head bowed low,
Remember the love we once shared;
    Miss me–but let me go.

For this is a journey we all must take
    And each must go alone,
It's all a part of the Master's plan
    A step on the road to home.
When you are lonely and sick at heart,
    Go to the friends we know
And bury your sorrow in doing good deeds.
Miss me - but let me go.

                   Author Unknown

UNTITLED I (10)

One or the other must leave,
One or the other must stay.
One or the other must grieve,
That is forever the way.

That is the vow that was sworn,
Faithful `til death do us part.
Braving what had to be borne,
Hiding the ache in the heart.

One, howsoever adored,
First must be summoned away.
That is the will of the Lord
One or the other must stay.

                Author Unknown

UNTITLED II

Now the laborer's task is over;
Now the battle day is past;
Now upon the farther shore
Lands the voyager at last.
Father, in Thy gracious keeping
Leaving we now thy servant sleeping.

John Ellerton

UNTITLED III

God saw you were getting tired
And a cure was not to be...
So he put his arms around you
And whispered "Come with Me."
With tearful eyes we watched you suffer
And saw you fade away.
Although we loved you dearly,
We could not make you stay.
A golden heart stopped beating;
A special man [woman] is put to rest.
God broke our hearts to prove to us
He only takes the Best.

Author Unknown

SECULAR

AFTERGLOW [i]

I'd like the memory of me to be a happy one,
I'd like to leave an afterglow of smiles when
    day is done.
I'd like to leave an echo
    whispering softly down the ways,
Of happy times and laughing times
    and bright and sunny days.
I'd like the tears of those who grieve
    to dry before the sun,
Of happy memories that I leave
    behind when day is done

Author Unknown

TURN AGAIN TO LIFE [ii]

If I should die and leave you
    here awhile,
Be not like others, sore undone,
    who keep
Long vigil by the silent dust
    and weep.
For my sake turn again to life
    and smile,
Nerving thy heart and trembling hand
    to do
That which will comfort other souls
    than thine;
Complete these dear unfinished tasks
    of mine,
And I, perchance, may therein
    comfort you.

Mary Lee Hall

THERE IS NO DEATH

I am standing upon the seashore.
A ship at my side spreads her white sails
to the morning breeze and starts for the blue ocean.
She is an object of beauty and strength
and I stand and watch her until at length
she hangs like a speck of white cloud
just where the sea and sky come to mingle
with each other.

Then someone at my side says, "There! She's Gone!"
Gone where? Gone from my sight, that's all.
She is just as large in mast and hull and spur
as she was when she left my side,
and she is just as able to bear her load of living weight
to her destined port.

Her diminished size is in me, not in her.
And just at that moment, when someone at my side says,
"There, she's gone," there are other eyes watching
her coming and other voices ready to take up the glad shout,
"There she comes!"
And that is dying.

Author Unknown

EACH LIFE IS A SONG

A life is like a song we write
    in our own tone and key.
Each life we touch reflects a note
    that forms the melody.
We choose the theme and chorus
    of the song to bear our name.
And each will have a special sound,
    no two can be the same.
So when someone we love departs,
    in memory we find
Their song plays on within the hearts
    of those they leave behind.
                Author Unknown

I'M NOT HERE [v]

Don't stand by my grave and weep
For I'm not there, I do not sleep
I am a thousand winds that blow
I am the diamond's glint on snow
I am the sunlight on ripened grain
I am the gentle autumn's rain.

When you awaken in the morning hush
I am the swift uplifting rush
Of quiet birds in circle flight
I am the soft stars that shine at night
Do not stand at my grave and cry
I am not there, I did not die.

Anonymous

RELEASE ME [vi]

When I am gone, release me, let me go
   I have so many things to see and do.
You mustn't tie yourself to me with tears
   Be thankful for our beautiful years.
I gave to you my love. You can only guess
   How much you gave to me in happiness.
I thank you for the love you have shown
   But now it's time I traveled alone.

So grieve awhile for me if grieve you must
   Then let your grief be comforted by trust.
It's only for a time that we must part
   So bless the memories within your heart.
I won't be far away, for life goes on
   And if you need me, call and I will come.
Though you can't see or touch me, I'll be near
   And if you listen with your heart you'll hear
   all of my love around you soft and clear.

And when you must come this way alone
   I'll greet you with a smile and say,
"Welcome Home!"

Author Unknown

BECACAUSE I COULD NOT STOP FOR DEATH

[vii]

Because I could not stop for Death,
He kindly stopped for me;
The carriage held but just ourselves
And Immortality.

Emily Dickinson

UNTITLED

[viii]

Tread lightly, she is near
Under the snow,
Speak gently, she can hear
The daisies grow.

Oscar Wilde

FINAL DISPOSITION/INTERMENT
Chapter 5

Unveil thy bosom, faithful tomb;
Take this new treasure to thy trust,
And give these sacred relics room
To slumber in the silent dust.

Dr. Isaac Watts

FINAL DISPOSITION ARRANGEMENTS

Many of today's funeral homes are located within or adjacent to cemeteries. If the chosen funeral home has such an affiliation, final disposition can be concurrent with funeral arrangements. The first decision is in choosing burial, entombment, or cremation.

The two disposition methods for casketed remains are ground burial or mausoleum entombment. A highly personal decision, families vary in disposition preferences. The decision process centers around *(a)* weather conditions during the disposition; *(b)* availability of space in a particular section of the cemetery; and *(c)* the cost factor—a mausoleum crypt is usually more expensive than ground burial.

Ground Burial
Decisions related to ground burial include selecting a specifically named garden or garden area with a special monument. Some sections of a cemetery require that the decedent belong to a special group such as a fraternity, have a religious affiliation, or be an American Veteran. Mostly, however, several options exist within cemeteries.

There are different types of ground burials such as single or multiple grave depth spaces. Consideration may also be given to location of the grave space to ensure ease of access for those attending the committal service, as well as for subsequent family visits.

Different costs are associated with ground burial. As a general rule, costs are increased when special monument or feature garden properties are selected.

Entombment
If the casketed remains are to be placed in a mausoleum, several choices are available. Cost, here, depends upon factors such as whether the selection is an enclosed mausoleum or outside crypt. Another is the vertical location. Crypts at chest or eye level when standing in front of them are the most expensive; the cost is *generally* reduced the higher the placement.

Some enclosed mausoleums are climate-controlled, especially in areas with extreme hot or cold seasons. As in ground burial, mausoleum crypts can be single or tandem. Many are side-by-side covered by a single piece of granite or marble. Private family mausoleums are also available in some cemeteries, typically much more expensive than community areas.

Perpetual Care

Both perpetual- and nonperpetual-care cemeteries exist, many older cemeteries belonging to the nonperpetual-care group. If the selection is a perpetual-care cemetery, a one-time fee will be charged when the property is purchased. This fee is collected for ground burial, entombment, or inurnment, then placed into a special trust account for perpetual maintenance of the property.

If it is a nonperpetual-care cemetery, the next of kin may be billed on a periodic basis for upkeep and maintenance. Virtually all new cemeteries offer perpetual care; some states regulate these applicable charges and deposit requirements, by law. The best value in a cemetery comes with the ability to pay a reasonable one-time fee, with no additional expense for maintenance.

Vaults

Just as many different components are used to construct caskets, various materials are used in the manufacture of burial vaults. Most common are concrete, fiberglass, and steel, lined or unlined. Lining creates a seal against the entrance of outside elements once the casket is placed into the vault. The primary purpose is to ensure that the ground does not settle atop the casket, causing it to collapse over time due to the weight of dirt and grass pressing directly onto it. The secondary reason is to ensure the casket is protected from ground elements such as water, which can cause corrosion over time.

While there are no laws requiring purchase of a vault, virtually every cemetery has a policy requiring use of a grave liner or vault. This is particularly true if the cemetery incorporates perpetual care.

Tent or Shelter

Many cemeteries provide a tent placed at the gravesite for the committal service. This protects against inclement weather for those attending. Standard practice includes chairs for the immediate family; the balance of attendees can stand under the tent. There is often an additional charge for use of a tent, and it is highly recommended that it be requested—if not offered.

Another option is to have the public service conclude at the end of the funeral service, then hold a private burial or entombment for immediate family only. In erratic climate areas, a sheltered place in the cemetery may be used for the committal service rather than gathering at the grave or mausoleum. These shelters provide greater protection against the elements than a tent, but still allow a committal service within the cemetery. Many such facilities include sound systems.

Casket Placement

It is customary to lower the casket into the ground, or to place it into the mausoleum crypt following the committal service only after family and friends have left the cemetery. It can be a traumatic experience to watch a casket lowered into the ground or placed into a crypt. Unless specially requested to see this done, the cemetery workers will wait until everyone has left before they complete the burial or entombment. For religious customs requiring the casket to be placed into the ground or crypt while the officiant and family are present, cemeteries willingly accommodate such traditions.

Memorial Markers

Memorial markers or monuments declare and honor the place of final disposition. A cemetery or supplier can be contracted to create a special monument. Size, shape, design, artwork, and wording on the finished product offer limitless possibilities. Monuments placed upright on the grave are typically granite, a marker which lies flat on the ground either granite or bronze. Most cemeteries impose a specific range of monument sizes to ensure the grounds appear as uniform as possible. Perpetual-care cemeteries often allow only flat markers due to costs associated with maintenance of upright monuments.

Cemeteries commonly prefer, or require, that bronze or granite markers be set into the ground so that the marker is flush with the grass. Floral vases can be incorporated within the marker, or a special container placed in the ground at the top of the marker.

Mausoleum crypts are usually limited to the name and dates of birth and death of the deceased. In some cases, a cross or other religious symbol, or a fraternal emblem is allowed on the front with the name bar. Most mausoleums will also permit an attached floral vase.

The marker can be purchased from the cemetery, funeral home, or a monument company. It is extremely important to know and understand the cemetery rules and procedures prior to ordering a marker or monument. If a marker or monument is purchased from an outside source, it must comply with these guidelines or possibly be barred from placement within the cemetery. (See Chapter 13 for *Memorial Markers/Headstones* examples.)

Floral Pieces

Most cemeteries are strict in their rules for flower placement. It is common practice to place flowers from the funeral service upon the grave or at the mausoleum crypt after conclusion of the services. They usually remain there a few days, and are then removed. They may be removed sooner—if they interfere with maintenance of the cemetery such as mowing the grass, or if they have wilted. Future placement usually requires a floral vase on the grave or vault. Some cemeteries allow artificial floral arrangements such as plastic or silk. Others permit only fresh flowers, which will be removed after they have wilted.

To repeat, it is important to learn the cemetery's rules and regulations to avoid future misunderstanding. Such guidelines are usually posted and/or made available upon request at the cemetery office.

Reserving Additional Space(s)

Most cemeteries allow families to reserve adjacent ground or mausoleum crypts or niches for a short time—to give family members the opportunity to purchase them if so desired. This practice helps keep costs as reasonable as possible at the time of death of a family member, but allows sufficient time following the initial grief period to decide on additional space. If the reservation is not exercised within the specified time indicated, however, the property returns to cemetery inventory. Note that it is possible to arrange a payment schedule to include such additional property purchase(s) during the initial funeral arrangements.

Cremains Disposition

Following the cremation process, the cremains can be returned to the next of kin (representative), or are prepared for placement within a cemetery or church. If next of kin elects to have the cremains scattered without further relocation, this can be arranged.

Cremated remains may be placed in a permanent public location, kept at home, placed on the private property of the family, or scattered in certain public areas such as the sea. It is strongly advised that families give careful consideration before electing to scatter the cremains to determine if that would be preferable to placing them in a permanent location to visit in the future. Many families who have already scattered cremains later purchase space within a cemetery for a place to go to reflect, or to pay respects on important holidays or anniversaries.

Cemeteries offer space within a columbarium (a structure designed with niches) or ground areas used for the placement of the cremains. If a columbarium space is selected, there are areas providing the display of urns, or where the urn or cremains container is concealed behind a granite or marble front. The cremains may also be placed into the grave of a spouse or family member—depending solely on the policies of the cemetery.

Billing and Payment

Today, cemetery arrangements are similar to those of funeral homes regarding product and service costs, including payment methods. It is also understood that a marker will not be ordered or set until the cemetery bill is paid in full. To make it more convenient for families, funeral homes will sometimes allow the cemetery expense to be added to their bill, and will advance a check for cemetery charges. This is an advantage when there is only one life insurance policy assigned to the funeral home for payment of all charges.

AMERICAN VETERANS' PRIVILEGES
Chapter 6

The American Flag

Flag of the free heart's hope and home,
*   By angel hands to valor given,*
Thy stars have lit the welkin dome,
*   And all thy hues were born in heaven.*
Forever float that standard sheet!
*   Where breathes the foe but falls before us,*
With Freedom's soil beneath our feet,
*   And Freedom's banner streaming o'er us!*
                                    Joseph Rodman Drake

VETERAN'S DEATH BENEFITS AND PRIVILEGES

Benefits available to qualified veterans have been dramatically reduced in recent years. There are still some available, however, which the funeral home can help to secure for the family. To receive any such benefits, the family must provide a copy of the DD214 (to the funeral home), which is proof of military discharge with detailed description of time served.

If the DD214 form cannot be located among the deceased veteran's belongings, a duplicate copy can be ordered from the local Veterans Administration Office. (See the form containing the necessary information to order the replacement DD214, *Request Pertaining to Military Records,* in this section.)

American Flag

In memory of service rendered to his/her country, every American veteran is entitled to an American flag displayed during a funeral or memorial service.

If the casket is present and open, the flag can be folded into traditional triangular form and placed in the head panel or at the head of the casket; or, it may be draped at the foot of the casket. If closed, the flag is either draped over it or placed at the head. If a spray of flowers is chosen to cover the casket, the flag cannot be draped there, but should be appropriately displayed.

It is well known to most Americans that the American flag used during funeral or memorial services is presented to the next of kin at the conclusion of any service held at the burial site.

What is less known is that if there is no burial ceremony, the flag may be presented to the next of kin ("or to a close friend or associate when no claim is made by next of kin") at any service location, or prior to the deceased being shipped out of the jurisdiction, naming just two possibilities. There are no set rules for this part of presentation.

(See *Application for United States Flag for Burial Purposes* form, and full instructions for the correct method of folding under *Use of Flag* form, at the end of this chapter.)

Military Honor Guard

The basic Honor Guard is for two members of a U.S. Army, Navy, Marines, Air Force, or Coast Guard Color Guard to fold and present the American flag to the next of kin. The military may also provide pallbearers (who will also ceremoniously assist in the folding of the flag); a bugler playing "Taps"; a 21-gun salute; and a military chaplain. This all depends on the military branch represented in the funeral or memorial service, and the availability of military personnel who volunteer for this duty on the requested day.

Burial

All American veterans are entitled to burial in a nationally recognized veterans' cemetery, at no "cemetery" costs to the family. The spouse is also entitled to be buried next to him/her when (s)he dies, also at no cemetery or marker costs. The second space must be reserved for the spouse *at the time of the first interment,* if requested by or on behalf of the spouse. While there is no charge for the interment of both the veteran and spouse in the cemetery, funeral home charges remain the responsibility of the family.

If final disposition is in a private cemetery, the Veterans Administration will pay a minimal amount towards the cost of the gravesite purchased.

Marker

A memorial grave marker is available to all veterans—regardless of location of interment. Whether interred in a veteran's, private, or municipal burial ground, the cemetery will order the marker for the family.

Further, the Veterans Administration will provide some reimbursement for a marker independently purchased by the family, but not for the spouse in this instance.

Many private cemeteries offer special prices for veterans and their spouses in sections reserved for veterans. (See *Illustrations of Standard Government Headstones and Markers,* plus pertinent applicable information, in this section.)

REQUEST PERTAINING TO MILITARY RECORDS

Please read instructions on the reverse. If more space is needed, use plain paper.

SECTION I—INFORMATION NEEDED TO LOCATE RECORDS (Furnish as much as possible)

1. NAME USED DURING SERVICE (Last, first, and middle)	2. SOCIAL SECURITY NO.	3. DATE OF BIRTH	4. PLACE OF BIRTH

5. ACTIVE SERVICE, PAST AND PRESENT   (For an effective records search, it is important that ALL service be shown below)

BRANCH OF SERVICE (Also, show last organization, if known)	DATES OF ACTIVE SERVICE — DATE ENTERED	DATE RELEASED	Check one OFFICER	EN-LISTED	SERVICE NUMBER DURING THIS PERIOD

6. RESERVE SERVICE, PAST OR PRESENT   If "none," check here ▶ ☐

a. BRANCH OF SERVICE	b. DATES OF MEMBERSHIP FROM	TO	c. Check one OFFICER	EN-LISTED	d. SERVICE NUMBER DURING THIS PERIOD
			☐	☐	

7. NATIONAL GUARD MEMBERSHIP   (Check one): ☐ a. ARMY   ☐ b. AIR FORCE   ☐ c. NONE

d. STATE	e. ORGANIZATION	f. DATES OF MEMBERSHIP FROM	TO	g. Check one OFFICER	EN-LISTED	h. SERVICE NUMBER DURING THIS PERIOD
				☐	☐	

8. IS SERVICE PERSON DECEASED ☐ YES ☐ NO   If "yes," enter date of death.

9. IS (WAS) INDIVIDUAL A MILITARY RETIREE OR FLEET RESERVIST ☐ YES ☐ NO

SECTION II—REQUEST

1. EXPLAIN WHAT INFORMATION OR DOCUMENTS YOU NEED; OR, CHECK ITEM 2; OR, COMPLETE ITEM 3		2. IF YOU ONLY NEED A STATEMENT OF SERVICE check here ☐

3. LOST SEPARA-TION DOCUMENT REPLACE-MENT REQUEST (Complete a or b, and c.)	a. REPORT OF SEPARATION (DD Form 214 or equivalent) ☐	YEAR ISSUED	This contains information normally needed to determine eligibility for benefits. It may be furnished only to the veteran, the surviving next of kin, or to a representative with veteran's signed release (item 5 of this form).
	b. DISCHARGE CERTIFICATE ☐	YEAR ISSUED	This shows only the date and character at discharge. It is of little value in determining eligibility for benefits. It may be issued only to veterans discharged honorably or under honorable conditions; or, if deceased, to the surviving spouse.
	c. EXPLAIN HOW SEPARATION DOCUMENT WAS LOST		

4. EXPLAIN PURPOSE FOR WHICH INFORMATION OR DOCUMENTS ARE NEEDED

6. REQUESTER

a. IDENTIFICATION (check appropriate box)

☐ Same person Identified in Section I   ☐ Surviving spouse

☐ Next of kin (relationship) _____

☐ Other (specify)

b. SIGNATURE (see instruction 3 on reverse side)	DATE OF REQUEST

5. RELEASE AUTHORIZATION, IF REQUIRED
(Read instruction 3 on reverse side)

I hereby authorize release of the requested information/documents to the person indicated at right (item 7).

VETERAN SIGN HERE ▶ _____

(If signed by other than veteran show relationship to veteran.)

7. Please type or print clearly —   COMPLETE RETURN ADDRESS

Name, number and street, city, State and ZIP code

TELEPHONE NO. (include area code) ▶

INSTRUCTIONS

1. Information needed to locate records. Certain identifying information is necessary to determine the location of an individual's record of military service. Please give careful consideration to and answer each item on this form. If you do not have and cannot obtain the information for an item, show "NA," meaning the information is "not available." Include as much of the requested information as you can. This will help us to give you the best possible service.

2. Charges for service. A nominal fee is charged for certain types of service. In most instances service fees cannot be determined in advance. If your request involves a service fee you will be notified as soon as that determination is made.

3. Restrictions on release of information. Information from records of military personnel is released subject to restrictions imposed by the military departments consistent with the provisions of the Freedom of Information Act of 1967 (as amended in 1974) and the Privacy Act of 1974. A service person has access to almost any information contained in his own record. The next of kin, if the veteran is deceased, and Federal officers for official purposes, are authorized to receive information from a military service or medical record only as specified in the above cited Acts. Other requesters must have the release authorization, in item 5 of the form, signed by the veteran or, if deceased, by the next of kin. Employers and others needing proof of military service are expected to accept the information shown on documents issued by the Armed Forces at the time a service person is separated.

4. Location of military personnel records. The various categories of military personnel records are described in the chart below. For each category there is a code number which indicates the address at the bottom of the page to which this request should be sent. For each military service there is a note explaining approximately how long the records are held by the military service before they are transferred to the National Personnel Records Center, St. Louis. Please read these notes carefully and make sure you send your inquiry to the right address. Please note especially that the record is not sent to the National Personnel Records Center as long as the person retains any sort of reserve obligation, whether drilling or non-drilling.

(If the person has two or more periods of service within the same branch, send your request to the office having the record for the last period of service.)

5. Definitions for abbreviations used below:
NPRC—National Personnel Records Center   PERS—Personnel Records
TDRL—Temporary Disability Retirement List   MED—Medical Records

SERVICE	NOTE: (See paragraph 4 above.)	CATEGORY OF RECORDS — WHERE TO WRITE	ADDRESS CODE ▼
AIR FORCE (USAF)	*Except for TDRL and general officers retired with pay, Air Force records are transferred to NPRC from Code 1, 90 days after separation and from Code 2, 150 days after separation.*	Active members (includes National Guard on active duty in the Air Force), TDRL, and general officers retired with pay.	1
		Reserve, retired reservist in nonpay status, current National Guard officers not on active duty in Air Force, and National Guard released from active duty in Air Force.	2
		Current National Guard enlisted not on active duty in Air Force.	13
		Discharged, deceased, and retired with pay.	14
COAST GUARD (USCG)	*Coast Guard officer and enlisted records are transferred to NPRC 7 months after separation.*	Active, reserve, and TDRL members.	3
		Discharged, deceased, and retired members *(see next item)*.	14
		Officers separated before 1/1/29 and enlisted personnel separated before 1/1/15.	6
MARINE CORPS (USMC)	*Marine Corps records are transferred to NPRC between 6 and 9 months after separation.*	Active, TDRL, and Selected Marine Corps Reserve members.	4
		Individual Ready Reserve and Fleet Marine Corps Reserve members.	5
		Discharged, deceased, and retired members *(see next item)*.	14
		Members separated before 1/1/1905.	6
ARMY (USA)	*Army records are transferred to NPRC as follows: Active Army and Individual Ready Reserve Control Groups: About 60 days after separation. U.S. Army Reserve Troop Unit personnel: About 120 to 180 days after separation.*	Reserve, living retired members, retired general officers, and active duty records of current National Guard members who performed service in the U.S. Army before 7/1/72.*	7
		Active officers (including National Guard on active duty in the U.S. Army).	8
		Active enlisted (including National Guard on active duty in the U.S. Army) and enlisted TDRL.	9
		Current National Guard officers not on active duty in the U.S. Army.	12
		Current National Guard enlisted not on active duty in the U.S. Army.	13
		Discharged and deceased members *(see next item)*.	14
		Officers separated before 7/1/17 and enlisted separated before 11/1/12.	6
		Officers and warrant officers TDRL.	8
NAVY (USN)	*Navy records are transferred to NPRC 6 months after retirement or complete separation.*	Active members (including reservists on duty)—PERS and MED	10
		Discharged, deceased, retired (with and without pay) less than six months, TDRL, drilling and nondrilling reservists — PERS ONLY	10
		(same) — MED ONLY	11
		Discharged, deceased, retired (with and without pay) more than six months *(see next item)*—PERS & MED	14
		Officers separated before 1/1/03 and enlisted separated before 1/1/1886—PERS and MED	6

Code 12 applies to active duty records of current National Guard officers who performed service in the U.S. Army after 6/30/72.
Code 13 applies to active duty records of current National Guard enlisted members who performed service in the U.S. Army after 6/30/72.

ADDRESS LIST OF CUSTODIANS (BY CODE NUMBERS SHOWN ABOVE)—Where to write / send this form for each category of records

1	Air Force Manpower and Personnel Center Military Personnel Records Division Randolph AFB, TX 78150-6001	**5**	Marine Corps Reserve Support Center 10950 El Monte Overland Park, KS 66211-1408	**8**	USA MILPERCEN ATTN: DAPC-MSR 200 Stoval Street Alexandria, VA 22332-0400	**12**	Army National Guard Personnel Center Columbia Pike Office Building 5600 Columbia Pike Falls Church, VA 22041
2	Air Reserve Personnel Center Denver, CO 80280-5000	**6**	Military Archives Division National Archives and Records Administration Washington, DC 20408	**9**	Commander U.S. Army Enlisted Records and Evaluation Center Ft. Benjamin Harrison, IN 46249-5301	**13**	The Adjutant General *(of the appropriate State, DC, or Puerto Rico)*
3	Commandant U.S. Coast Guard Washington, DC 20593-0001	**7**	Commander U.S. Army Reserve Personnel Center ATTN: DARP-PAS 9700 Page Boulevard St. Louis, MO 63132-5200	**10**	Commander Naval Military Personnel Command ATTN: NMPC-036 Washington, DC 20370-5036	**14**	National Personnel Records Center (Military Personnel Records) 9700 Page Boulevard St. Louis, MO 63132
4	Commandant of the Marine Corps (Code MMRB-10) Headquarters, U.S. Marine Corps Washington, DC 20380-0001			**11**	Naval Reserve Personnel Center New Orleans, LA 70146-5000		

Department of Veterans Affairs

APPLICATION FOR UNITED STATES FLAG FOR BURIAL PURPOSES

RESPONDENT BURDEN: VA may not conduct or sponsor, and respondent is not required to respond to this collection of information unless it displays a valid OMB Control Number. Public reporting burden for this collection of information is estimated to average 15 minutes per response, including the time for reviewing instructions, searching existing data sources, gathering and maintaining the data needed, and completing and reviewing the collection of information. If you have comments regarding this burden estimate or any other aspect of this collection of information, call 1-800-827-1000 for mailing information on where to send your comments.

IMPORTANT - Postmaster or other issuing official: Submit this form to the nearest VA Regional Office. Be sure to complete the stub at the bottom.

1. LAST NAME - FIRST NAME-MIDDLE NAME OF DECEASED (Print or type)

2. BRANCH OF SERVICE (Check box)

☐ ARMY ☐ NAVY ☐ AIR FORCE ☐ MARINE CORPS ☐ COAST GUARD

☐ OTHER (Specify)

3. VETERAN'S SERVICE (Check box)

☐ SPANISH AMERICAN ☐ WWI ☐ WWII ☐ KOREAN CONFLICT ☐ AFTER 1-31-55 ☐ VIETNAM ERA

☐ OTHER (Specify)

4. CONDITION UNDER WHICH VETERAN WAS RELEASED FROM SERVICE (Check box) (See Item 2, Instructions on Reverse)

☐ A. VETERAN OF A WAR, MEXICAN BORDER SERVICE, OR OF SERVICE AFTER 1-31-55, DISCHARGED OR RELEASED FROM ACTIVE DUTY UNDER CONDITIONS OTHER THAN DISHONORABLE

☐ B. DISCHARGED FROM OR RELEASED FROM ACTIVE DUTY IN U.S. ARMED FORCES UNDER CONDITIONS OTHER THAN DISHONORABLE, AFTER SERVING AT LEAST ONE ENLISTMENT, OR DISCHARGED FOR DISABILITY INCURRED IN LINE OF DUTY

☐ C. BY DEATH IN ACTIVE SERVICE AFTER MAY 27, 1941, AND FLAG NOT FURNISHED BY THE SERVICE DEPARTMENT

☐ D. SEPARATED FROM PHILIPPINE MILITARY FORCES, UNDER CONDITIONS OTHER THAN DISHONORABLE, AFTER SERVING WITH THE UNITED STATES IN SUCH FORCES UNDER THE PRESIDENT'S ORDER OF JULY 26, 1941, AND DIED ON OR AFTER APRIL 25, 1951

5. NAME OF PERSON ENTITLED TO RECEIVE FLAG

6. ADDRESS OF PERSON ENTITLED TO RECEIVE FLAG

7. RELATIONSHIP TO DECEASED (See Item 1, Instructions on Reverse)

PERSONAL DATA OF DECEASED (To be completed if possible)

8. VA FILE NUMBER

9. SOCIAL SECURITY NUMBER

10. SERVICE SERIAL NUMBER

11. DATE OF ENLISTMENT

12. DATE OF DISCHARGE

13. DATE OF BIRTH

14. DATE OF DEATH

15. DATE OF BURIAL

16. PLACE OF BURIAL (Name of cemetery, city, and State)

17. REMARKS

I CERTIFY that, to the best of my knowledge and belief, the statements made above are correct and true, the deceased is eligible, in accordance with instructions on reverse for issue of a United States flag for burial purposes, and such flag has not previously been applied for or furnished.

18. SIGNATURE OF APPLICANT (Sign in INK)

19. ADDRESS OF APPLICANT (Number and street or rural route, city or P.O., and ZIP Code)

20. RELATIONSHIP TO DECEASED

21. DATE SIGNED

PENALTY - The law provides that whoever makes any statement of a material fact knowing it to be false shall be punished by a fine or both imprisonment or both.

ACKNOWLEDGMENT OF RECEIPT OF FLAG

I CERTIFY that the flag requested by the applicant will be used to drape the casket of the deceased in whose honor it is issued by the Department of Veterans Affairs; and that Item 6 of the Instructions will be complied with.

SIGNATURE OF PERSON RECEIVING FLAG (Sign in INK)

DATE FLAG RECEIVED

NAME AND ADDRESS OF POST OFFICE OR OTHER FLAG ISSUE POINT

FOR VA USE

DATE NOTIFICATION FORWARDED TO SUPPLY

INITIALS OF RESPONSIBLE VA EMPLOYEE

VA FORM
SEP 1999 **21-2008**

EXISTING STOCK OF VA FORM 2008, SEP 1993(R), WILL BE USED.

This stub is to be completed by the POSTMASTER or other issuing official. Upon receipt the VA Regional Office will detach and forward it to the appropriate Supply Officer.

NOTIFICATION OF ISSUANCE OF FLAG

DATE FLAG ISSUED

SIGNATURE OF POSTMASTER OR OTHER ISSUING OFFICIAL

ADDRESS OF POST OFFICE OR OTHER FLAG ISSUE POINT

FOR VA USE ►

DATE OF REPLACEMENT

VA FORM
SEP 1999 **21-2008**

EXISTING STOCK OF VA FORM 2008, SEP 1993(R), WILL BE USED.

SEE REVERSE

INSTRUCTIONS

1. No flag may be issued unless a completed application form has been received (38 U.S.C. 901). The person filling out the application must state (under "relationship to deceased") whether he/she is: *(a)* A relative, and degree of relationship (e.g., "Brother"); *(b)* the funeral director; *(c)* a representative of veterans' or other organization having charge of the burial (e.g., "The American Legion"); *(d)* other person having a knowledge of the facts, and acting in the interest of the deceased or his/her family (e.g., "Friend"; "Det. Clerk").

2. One of the numbered conditions listed "under which deceased was separated from service" must be evidenced, normally by a document such as a discharge paper, before a flag may be issued.

(a) The phrase "veteran of a war" (No. 1) requires a showing that the deceased was in service in the United States armed forces during a war period. The phrase "Mexican border service" means active service during the period beginning on January 1, 1911, and ending on April 5, 1917, in Mexico, on the borders thereof, or in the waters adjacent thereto. The phrase "service after January 31, 1955" relates to veterans with active military, naval, or air service after the date.

(b) The phrase "under conditions other than dishonorable" requires a showing of discharge or release from active duty under honorable conditions ("Honorable" or "General") from the indicated period of service in the United States armed forces, or, in absence of such discharge or release from active duty, a determination by Department of Veterans Affairs that discharge or release from active duty, was under conditions other than dishonorable.

(c) The phrase "at least one enlistment" (No. 2) is construed to include service of a commissioned officer whose service, computed from date of entrance into commissioned status to date of separation from service, terminated under honorable conditions, and in all cases, relates to peacetime service before June 27, 1950.

(d) When the deceased was honorably discharged for disability, it may be assumed that the disability was "incurred in line of duty."

(e) Issue of flag in in-service cases (No. 3) is required only when deceased was interred outside the United States, or remains not recovered, or where service department cannot supply flag in time for burial. Explanation should be included under "Remarks."

3. When the applicant is unable to furnish documentary proof, such as a discharge under honorable conditions ("Honorable" or "General"), an application may be accepted and a flag issued when statement is made by a person of established character and reputation that he/she personally knows the deceased to have been a veteran of a war, the Mexican border service, or of service after January 31, 1955, discharged or released from active duty, under honorable conditions, or to have been a person discharged from, or released from active duty in the United States Army, Navy, Air Force, Marine Corps, or Coast Guard under honorable conditions after serving at least one complete peacetime enlistment, before June 27, 1950, or for disability incurred in line of duty; or that the deceased was in active service at the time of death and a flag was not obtainable from a military or naval establishment in time for burial.

4. The following classes of persons are ineligible for issue of a burial flag:

(a) A discharged or rejected draftee, or a member of the National Guard, who reported to camp in answer to the President's call for World War I service but who, when medically examined, was not finally accepted for military service.

(b) A person who was discharged from World War I service prior to November 12, 1918, on his/her own application or solicitation, by reason of being an alien, or any person discharged for alienage during a period of hostilities.

(c) A person who served with any of the forces allied with the United States in any war, even though a United States citizen, if he/she did not serve with the United States armed forces.

(d) A person inducted for training and service who, before entering upon such training and service, was transferred to the Enlisted Reserve Corps and given a furlough.

(e) A former temporary member of the United States Coast Guard Reserve.

(f) A reservist who served only on active duty for training unless he/she was disabled or died from a disease or injury incurred or aggravated in line of duty.

5. Flags will not be issued subsequent to burial, except where circumstances render it impossible to obtain a flag in time to drape the casket of a deceased veteran prior to final interment. The applicant must personally sign the application and include (under "Remarks") a statement explaining the circumstances preventing the requesting of a burial flag prior to final interment.

6. *(a)* The flag will be disposed of as follows: When actually used to drape the casket of the deceased, it must be delivered to the next of kin (or to a close friend or associate when no claim is made by next of kin) following interment or inurnment. If there is no living relative, or one cannot be located, and no friend or associate requests the flag, it must be returned to the nearest Department of Veterans Affairs.

(b) The phrase "next of kin," for the purpose of disposing of the flag, is defined as follows with preference to entitlement in the order listed below:

(1) Widow or widower.

(2) Children, according to age (minor child may be issued a flag on application signed by guardian).

(3) Parents, including adoptive, stepparents, and foster parents.

(4) Brothers or sisters, including brothers or sisters of the halfblood.

(5) Uncles or aunts.

(6) Nephews or nieces.

(7) Others - cousins, grandparents, etc.

(c) The phrase "close friend or associate" means any person who establishes by evidence that he/she was a close friend or an associate of the deceased.

GENERAL INFORMATION SHEET

APPLICATION FOR STANDARD GOVERNMENT HEADSTONE OR MARKER
FOR INSTALLATION IN A PRIVATE OR STATE VETERANS' CEMETERY

RESPONDENT BURDEN - Public reporting burden for this collection of information is estimated to average one-fourth hour per response, including the time for reviewing instructions, searching existing data sources, gathering and maintaining the data needed, and completing and reviewing the collection of information. Send comments regarding this burden estimate or any other aspect of this collection of information, including suggestions for reducing this burden to the VA Clearance Officer (045A4), 810 Vermont Avenue, NW, Washington, DC 20420. Please DO NOT send applications for benefits to this address.

BENEFIT PROVIDED

a. HEADSTONE OR MARKER - Furnished upon application for the **unmarked grave** of any deceased veteran. Applicant must certify the grave is **unmarked** and a Government headstone or marker is preferred to a privately purchased headstone or marker. This restriction applies to companion markers. Companion markers identify two or more decedents buried, or to be buried, in the same or adjoining graves. A grave is considered marked if a monument displays the decedent's name and dates of birth and/or death, even though the veteran's military data is not shown. Applicant may be anyone having knowledge of the deceased.

b. MEMORIAL HEADSTONE OR MARKER - Furnished upon application by a relative recognized as the next of kin for installation only in a cemetery to commemorate any veteran whose remains have not been recovered or identified, were buried at sea, donated to science, or cremated and the remains scattered; may not be used as a memento. Check box in block 2 and explain in block 27.

WHO IS ELIGIBLE - Any deceased veteran discharged under conditions other than dishonorable. To expedite processing, attach a copy of the deceased veteran's discharge certificate or a copy of other official document(s) pertaining to military service, if available. **Do not send original documents;** they will not be returned. Service after September 7, 1980, must be for a minimum of 24 months or be completed under special circumstances, e.g., death on active duty. Persons who have only limited active duty service for training while in the National Guard or Reserves are not eligible unless there are special circumstances, e.g., death while on, or as a result of training. Persons with extended Reserve or National Guard service which entitled them to retirement pay subsequent to October 27, 1992, are eligible; a copy of the Reserve Retirement Eligibility Benefits Letter must accompany the application. Active duty service during the Persian Gulf War for all referenced above also establishes eligibility. Service prior to World War I requires detailed documentation, e.g., muster rolls, extracts from State files, military or State organization where served, pension or land warrant, etc.

HOW TO APPLY - Mail the original only of the completed application (VA Form 40-1330) to:

Memorial Programs Service (403A)
Department of Veterans Affairs
810 Vermont Avenue, NW.
Washington, DC 20420-0001

The person or organization shown in block 19, Consignee should receive the headstone or marker within 70 days after we receive a fully completed application with correct information. Omissions or errors on the application will delay its processing and delay marking the veteran's grave.

The copy is for your records. A Government headstone or marker may only be furnished if a fully completed application form has been received.

SIGNATURES REQUIRED - The applicant, next of kin or other responsible person, signs in block 15, obtains the signature of consignee in block 22 and cemetery official in block 24. If there is no official on duty at the cemetery write "NONE" in block 24. State Veterans' Cemeteries are not required to complete blocks: 15, 16, 22 and 23.

ASSISTANCE NEEDED - If assistance is needed to complete this application, contact the nearest VA Regional Office, national cemetery, or a local veterans' organization. No fee should be paid in connection with the preparation of this application. Use block 27 for any clarification or information you wish to provide. Should you have special questions when filling out this form, please telephone our Applicant Assistance Division toll free at: 1-800-697-6947.

INSTALLATION - All costs to install the headstone or marker must be paid from private funds.

TRANSPORTATION - The headstone or marker is shipped without charge to the consignee, designated in block 19 of the application. The consignee must have a full street address; **delivery cannot be made to a Post Office Box.** An address showing Rural Route Delivery must include a daytime telephone number in block 20 to obtain delivery. An insufficient address may result in a nondeliverable headstone or marker.

*CAUTION - After completing the application, **please check carefully** to be sure you have accurately furnished all required information, thereby avoiding delays in marking the gravesite. Mistakes cannot be corrected after a headstone or marker has been ordered. Headstones or markers furnished remain the property of the United States Government and may not be used for any purpose other than to honor the memory of the decedent for whom the headstone or marker is issued. A Government provided headstone or marker may not be used as a footstone or to supplement a private monument, or be affixed to an existing inscribed monument.*

DETACH AND RETAIN THIS GENERAL INFORMATION SHEET AND THE COPY OF THE APPLICATION FOR YOUR RECORDS

VA FORM
JAN 1998(R) **40-1330**

USE OF THE FLAG

1. This flag is issued on behalf of the Department of Veterans Affairs to honor the memory of one who has served our country.

2. When used to drape the casket, the flag should be placed as follows:

(a) Closed Casket. - When the flag is used to drape a closed casket, it should be so placed that the union (blue field) is at the head and over the left shoulder of the deceased.

(b) Half Couch (Open). - When the flag is used to drape a half-couch casket, it should be placed in three layers to cover the closed half of the casket in such a manner that the blue field will be

the top fold, next to the open portion of the casket on the deceased's left.

(c) Full Couch (Open). - When the flag is used to drape a full-couch casket, it should be folded in a triangular shape and placed in the center part of the head panel of the casket cap, just above the left shoulder of the deceased.

3. During a military commitment ceremony, the flag which was used to drape the casket is held waist high over the grave by the pallbearers and, immediately after the sounding of "Taps," is folded in accordance with the paragraph below.

4. Folding the flag (see illustration):

CORRECT METHOD OF FOLDING THE UNITED STATES FLAG

(a) Fold the lower striped section of the flag over the blue field.

(c) A triangular fold is then started by bringing the stripe corner of the folded edge to the open edge.

(d) Outer point is then turned inward parallel with the open edge to form a second triangle.

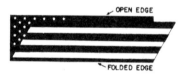

(b) Folded edge is then folded over to meet the open edge.

(e) Triangular folding is continued until the entire length of the flag is folded in the triangular shape of a cocked hat with only the blue field visible.

5. The flag should not be lowered into the grave or allowed to touch the ground. When taken from the casket, it should be folded as above.

6. The flag should form a distinctive feature of the ceremony of unveiling a statue or monument, but it should never be used as a covering for the statue or monument.

7. The flag should never be fastened, displayed, used, or stowed in such a manner as will permit it to be easily torn, soiled, or damaged in any way.

8. The flag should never have placed upon it, nor any part of it, nor attached to it, any mark, insignia, letter, word, figure, design, picture, or drawing of any nature.

9. The flag should never be used as a receptacle for receiving, holding, carrying, or delivering anything.

10. The flag, when badly worn, torn, or soiled should no longer be publicly displayed, but privately destroyed by burning in such a manner as to convey no suggestion of disrespect or irreverence.

ILLUSTRATIONS OF STANDARD GOVERNMENT HEADSTONES AND MARKERS

FLAT MARKERS

BRONZE

UPRIGHT HEADSTONE
WHITE MARBLE OR
LIGHT GRAY GRANITE

BRONZE NICHE

This niche marker is 8-1/2 inches long, 5-1/2 inches wide, with 7/16 inches rise. Weight is approximately 3 pounds; mounting bolts and washers are furnished with the marker. For use if entombment is in a columbarium or mausoleum, but not to supplement a private monument.

This grave marker is 24 inches long, 12 inches wide, with 3/4 inch rise. Weight is approximately 18 pounds. Anchor bolts, nuts and washers for fastening to a base are furnished with the marker. The base is not furnished by the Government.

LIGHT GRAY GRANITE OR WHITE MARBLE

This headstone is 42 inches long, 13 inches wide, and 4 inches thick. Weight is approximately 230 pounds. Variations may occur in stone color, and the marble may contain light to moderate veining.

This grave marker is 24 inches long, 12 inches wide, and 4 inches thick. Weight is approximately 130 pounds. Variations may occur in stone color; the marble may contain light to moderate veining.

NOTE: In addition to the headstone and markers illustrated, two special styles of upright marble headstones and flat markers are available to mark the graves of - those who served with the Union Forces, Civil War, or during the Spanish-American War; and those who served with the Confederate Forces, Civil War. Request should be made in block 27 of the application. It is necessary to submit detailed documentation which supports eligibility.

INSCRIPTION INFORMATION

MANDATORY ITEMS of inscription at Government expense are: Name, Branch of Service, Year of Birth, and Year of Death. Branches of Service are: U.S. Army, U.S. Navy, U.S. Air Force, U.S. Marine Corps, U.S. Coast Guard, and by exception, U.S. Army Air Corps, and other parent organizations authorized for certain periods of time. Different examples of inscription formats are illustrated above; **deviations in data sequence are not permitted.** More than one branch of service is permitted, subject to space availability.

OPTIONAL ITEMS which may be inscribed at Government expense, indicated by shaded title blocks are: military grade, rate or rank, war service, month and day of the dates of birth and death, an authorized emblem reflective of one's belief, and the valor awards and the Purple Heart listed in block 8. If any of these items are desired the information must be shown clearly in the shaded title blocks; documentation of the awards must accompany the application.

RESERVED SPACE for future inscription at private expense, such as spousal or dependent data may be authorized below the standard inscription if requested in block 27. Only two lines of space may be reserved on flat markers due to space limitations. Reserved space is unnecessary on upright marble or granite headstones as the reverse side is available for future inscriptions.

MEMORIAL HEADSTONES AND MARKERS (remains are not buried). The words "In Memory of" are mandatory and precede the authorized inscription data. The words "In Memory of" are not inscribed when remains are buried.

ADDITIONAL ITEMS may be inscribed, at Government expense, **subject to VA approval,** below the standard inscription and subject to space limitations. Some additional inscription items may, of necessity, be placed on the rear of the headstone. Such items may be terms of endearment, nicknames (not unseemly in nature) in expressions such as OUR BELOVED POPPY, LOVINGLY CALLED DUTCH, representations of military and civilian participation or accomplishment, and titles such as DOCTOR, REVEREND, etc. These requests should be made in block 27. Except for the Medal of Honor and authorized emblems of belief, no graphics, emblems or pictures are permitted on government monuments.

INCOMPLETE OR INACCURATE INFORMATION ON THE APPLICATION MAY RESULT IN ITS RETURN TO THE APPLICANT, A DELAY IN RECEIPT OF THE HEADSTONE OR MARKER, OR AN INCORRECT INSCRIPTION.

OBITUARIES
Chapter 7

PUBLISHED OBITUARY

Standard Newspaper Obituary Notice
Some community newspapers still publish obituary notices at no charge to the survivor(s) of the deceased. Those which do not charge generally specify what may be included in the obituary. A newspaper's circulation and geographic coverage usually dictates a charge or no-charge insertion; however, the pricing policy is at the option of each newspaper publisher.

In addition to the decedent's name, birth data, etc., this obituary usually includes service location(s), club or organization membership(s), occupation or career field, and a list of immediate-family survivors.

Extended Optional Notice
At the option of a newspaper, a brief article may be added to an obituary notice if the deceased lived in the community for a significant period, and/or was active in civic or political affairs.

If the decedent was a public figure, the newspaper might choose to print a photo with the notice, becoming more of a public interest story. This also depends on the size of the community newspaper.

Personalized Notice
Another type of obituary is one written by/for a family (with or without a photo) that includes as much information in as many words as they are willing to pay for—which can become expensive.

Other Publication Obituaries
Affiliate publications such as professional, business, club, or other newsletters may also want to enlighten their membership as to the death of one of its members, and may be notified, offering much the same data as newspapers, except for possible added human interest related to such associations of the deceased. These may also either be paid for (if specific inclusions are requested) or at no charge.

Following is a list of information most often requested by newspapers that publish obituaries which may, at least initially, serve as well for other types of publications such as professional journals, organizational publications, newsletters, and so forth.

MINIMUM INFORMATION NEEDED FOR ANY OBITUARY

First, middle, and last name of deceased
Month, day, and year of death
Location of death (residence, hospital, etc.)
City and state of death

City and state of birth
Month, day, and year of birth

Was deceased a veteran? What branch of service? Was service during a war?

First and last name of spouse and city of residence
First and last name(s) of child(ren) and city(ies) of residence
First and last name(s) of parent(s) and city(ies) of residence
First and last name(s) of brother(s) and city(ies) of residence
First and last name(s) of sister(s) and city(ies) of residence
Number of grandchildren
Number of great-grandchildren

When deceased moved to community of residence
Lodge, club, and civic organization affiliation(s)
Business career
Name of last employer, or of company owned

Month, day, and time of visitation period(s)
Name and address of funeral home
Month, day, time, and address of funeral or memorial service
Interment location

Selected charity or organization donation in lieu of flowers, if desired

Note: Typically, survivorship information will include only living relatives in a Standard Obituary. However, in some selected instances, if considered newsworthy by the publication, names of deceased relatives may also be included.

FOLLOWING THE SERVICE(S)
Chapter 8

AFTER-SERVICE RECEPTION

While gathering after a funeral or memorial service is more traditional than socially obligatory, many families take this opportunity to informally join with friends to remember the deceased.

It should be noted that some ethnic and societal groups use a *wake* for this purpose, that is, festivities held while keeping watch over the deceased—during the viewing before services and final disposition.

Location for After-service Gathering
The most common practice is to invite those attending the service to a family member's home. It is equally acceptable to use the social hall of a church or community center, or a restaurant which will provide adequate space and time span for all to comfortably socialize.

Whom to Invite
It is most appropriate, and simple, to invite everyone attending the service. It is especially important to ensure that friends who have traveled from other locations are advised of the gathering, in advance, and that a map or written information is made available—unless transportation is provided.

Not everyone attending the service will choose, or be able, to attend the gathering; some will stop by only briefly to demonstrate their support and friendship.

Catered or Potluck
The bereaved's friends often wish to be of assistance. Some church and social groups do an excellent job of organizing and assigning food to be prepared for this occasion. It is no less acceptable to hire a caterer to assume full responsibility.

Chips and dips, small finger foods, or light desserts such as a cookie tray are equally sufficient. Beverages can be alcoholic or nonalcoholic, coffee and tea, and/or soft drinks, depending solely on family preferences.

The support a family receives is more important than what is served at the gathering.

SOME AVAILABLE BENEFITS
Chapter 9

BENEFITS

There are always questions, and often mistaken opinions, relative to benefits immediately available for funeral services and disposition. From a partial benefit all the way to the full payment of selected services are possible. It is important to have a general understanding, or at least some idea, of what benefit options are within the realm of possibility. This should be discussed during the arrangement conference so that there is no misunderstanding as to how payment will be handled.

Social Security
Social Security benefits have been dramatically reduced in the last few years. A basic death benefit is paid to the surviving spouse of a decedent if the couple was living together at the time of death. This benefit cannot be assigned to or paid directly to the funeral home.

For individuals already drawing (or eligible for) social security benefits, the next of kin (or legally designated representative) must make an appointment with the nearest Social Security Administration office to discuss the changes in or eligibility  for benefits. Since it can take up to ten weeks to receive such benefits, the appointment should be made as soon as it is convenient following the death. In some cases, a telephone interview may suffice. The funeral director will provide the necessary notification paperwork by completing a "Statement of Death by Funeral Director" form, which (s)he will then forward directly to the Social Security Administration.

Veteran's Administration
Most families know little or nothing about benefits offered by the Veterans Administration for an honorably discharged, deceased veteran. This subject is addressed in detail in Chapter 6, *American Veterans' Privileges.*

Accident or Work-related Death
Funds are often provided for the chosen funeral/memorial services and final disposition when an accidental death occurs or when the cause is work-related. Insurance companies sometimes furnish funds if their insured party is in any way liable for the death such as an automobile malfunction, or an accident on the premises of the insured (restaurant, store, etc.). Further, each state has its own worker compensation laws which specifically cover employees who are injured and die as the result of a work-related accident.

The funeral home will likely be familiar with local and state policies relative to accidental death. If an insurance (or individually liable) company chooses to provide immediate assistance to the family of the deceased, it will inform the funeral home of what funds are available for services and disposition.

If litigation is anticipated, however, costs incurred by the death are generally involved in the suit, and expenses would need to be advanced by the family. Rarely will a funeral home or cemetery wait to be paid pending the outcome of a lawsuit.

Unions

Benefits are occasionally accessible to assist with the services and disposition if the deceased was an active union member (most often a person currently employed in an occupation covered by his or her union). Benefits may also be offered to a retired or unemployed union member, as long as dues are current and (s)he meets the criteria for membership. Most unions offer a reduced benefit package to retirees or those unemployed members at the time of death. All unions have human resource directors to assist families with such benefits. The funeral home will likely be familiar with local union benefits.

Life Insurance

A life insurance policy is a frequent method of payment for service and final disposition arrangements. The policy is usually assigned to the funeral home or cemetery for the amount of agreed-upon charges. The insurance company sends the funeral home (or cemetery) the payment authorized by the policy's beneficiary, then pays the proceeds balance, if any, directly to that heir. The funeral home to which the insurance is guaranteed then often pays other cash-advance items such as cemetery charges, floral arrangements, death certificates, family cars for the services, clergy offerings, etc.

State, County, or City Assistance

If there is no known next of kin, or if the next of kin does not reside in the area where the death has occurred, indigent-care funds from the state, county, or city may finance the funeral or memorial service and disposition of the deceased. The same funds may be obtainable for a family without the financial means to pay such costs. The funeral home can direct the family to the proper entity to apply for assistance. As a general rule, if assistance is applied for and granted, family members are not responsible for any of the financial arrangements. This will likely delay the services and disposition for several days, however, while the application is being processed.

CASKET SELECTION
Chapter 10

CASKET COMPONENTS

One definition for casket is a small box crafted with rich materials, often used to house jewels. A word often interchanged with casket is coffin. A coffin is generally a large oblong box in which some highly esteemed entity, such as a deceased person, is buried.

Keeping the definition in mind, the following lists the types of materials used for burial caskets, and reasons for the wide range of pricing. Materials typically used for casket construction are precious metals such as bronze and copper, stainless steel, steel, and wood.

Design, hardware, interior materials (fabrics), cathodic protection, protective vs nonprotective caskets, themes, as well as rentals, offer more options and are reflected in their costs.

Bronze

This nonrusting material is the most durable of all materials used in this construction. Because of its extreme durability and nonrusting nature, many park statues and monuments are crafted in bronze.

Bronze caskets are made of either 32- or 48-ounce thickness (weight classifications in which: 32-ounce bronze materials comprise 32 ounces per square foot; or, 48-ounce bronze material containing 48 ounces per square foot).

Cost is generally based on thickness of the metal, interior materials used, and design.

Copper

Also a nonrusting material. Although not as unyielding as bronze, copper is highly durable. The Statue of Liberty is made of copper with a steel structure. Several years ago, the steel portions of the State of Liberty required renovation as the result of rust from environmental exposure. The copper exterior remained in perfect condition.

Copper caskets, too, are either 32- or 48-ounce thickness. Weight classifications are identical to bronze caskets (as explained above).

Many families select copper over bronze caskets because, while offering the durability of precious metal, copper is considerably less expensive.

Stainless Steel

Well known for its hardiness, stainless steel is used in medical equipment, jet engines, skyscraper construction, and tableware. It is an alloy available in various grades, depending on the percentage of chromium used. The primary reason for using stainless steel for casket construction is its rust-resistant qualities.

Steel

Steel caskets are made primarily from three different gauges (or thicknesses). The thickest are 16-gauge; but they are also constructed of 18- and 20-gauge steel.

Gauge refers to how many sheets of metal it takes, when laid on top of each other, to equal an inch of thickness. For example, 20-gauge requires 20 pieces of metal placed together to equal one inch of thickness, while only 16 pieces of 16-gauge equals one inch. The lower the gauge number, the thicker the metal. As further reference, automobiles are built with less than 20-gauge steel. The thinnest metal ever used in the construction of caskets is 20-gauge.

Wood

Wood caskets can be hardwood or softwood. Hardwood comes from a leaf-bearing tree; softwood from a needle- or cone-bearing tree. Hardwood caskets are constructed of mahogany, walnut, cherry wood, maple, pecan, oak, or poplar. Softwood caskets are typically made of pine.

Prices vary depending upon the availability of the wood species and the labor involved to craft the casket. The strength and hardness of the wood can increase the labor involved to finish the product. Many families select wood because of its natural impression of warmth and beauty. The least expensive caskets manufactured today are of either plywood or pressed wood, covered with cloth.

CASKET DESIGNS

Caskets are designed with rounded or square corners. They also have differing sides such as flat, rounded, or containing an urn design. Lids are structured to lift in one or two sections. Those formed with one-piece lids are called "Full Couch" caskets; two-pieced lids are "Perfection-cut" or "Half Couch" caskets.

Hardware
A wide selection of hardware is available for caskets. The most common handles are full-length. They are either "stationary" (nonmovable) or "swing bar" (movable). There are also individual handles which may be stationary or swing bar.

Interior Material
Velvet, crepe, and twill are most commonly used in caskets. The most expensive is velvet, the least being twill.

Today, many designs are used in the head panel. Computers have opened the way to create a wide variety of phrases, artwork, or pictures for the casket interior. Another wide-ranging option is use of colors.

Cathodic Protection
This is a rust-inhibiting method used to protect steel from rust and corrosion—up to 2 1/2 times its natural life. A bar made of special magnesium alloy installed in caskets offers cathodic protection. It is the same process used for buried steel pipelines, ship hulls, water heaters, and numerous other steel items that come in contact with water and other corrosive elements.

Protective vs Nonprotective
A rubber gasket can provide protection against entrance of any outside element, such as water or bugs. All bronze, copper, stainless steel, and most steel caskets are likely to be protective. Wood caskets are nonprotective since wood is permeable, and therefore, does not provide complete protection from outside elements. Caskets providing protection are generally more expensive than those which do not.

Religious-themed
The most common "religious caskets" used are for Jewish burials. Constructed of wood, they contain no metal parts. These caskets are constructed of various woods, conjoined with dowel pegs and glue.

There are other religious-themed caskets such as those portraying "The Last Supper" in the head panel, or exterior hardware crafted to depict religious icons or ceremonies.

Rentals

Some funeral homes rent caskets for cremation services. This allows the deceased to be viewed during visitation and/or the funeral in a more pleasing casket. Most rental caskets are made of hardwood with a cremation container placed inside. After the service, the cremation container holding the deceased is removed and taken to the crematory.

A new cremation container is then placed into the hardwood casket shell for future rental. This offers fine quality at a reasonable price, eliminating the outright purchase of an expensive casket to be used only briefly.

> *Only waiting till the shadows*
> *Are a little longer grown,*
> *Only waiting till the glimmer*
> *Of the day's last beam is flown.*
> *Then from out the gathered darkness,*
> *Holy, deathless stars shall rise,*
> *By whose light my soul shall gladly*
> *Tread its pathway to the skies.*
>
> Anonymous

CASKET PICTURES AND DESCRIPTIONS

PROTECTIVE CASKET
(Metal)

Casket Type
        Full Couch (casket lid made of one piece)

Exterior Materials
        Bronze, 48- or 32-ounce
        Copper, 48- or 32-ounce

Interior Materials
        Velvet

PROTECTIVE CASKET
(Metal)

Casket
    Half Couch or Perfection-cut (casket lid opens in two pieces)

Exterior Materials
    Stainless Steel
    Steel, 16-, 18-, or 20-gauge

Interior Materials
    Velvet
    Crepe
    Twill

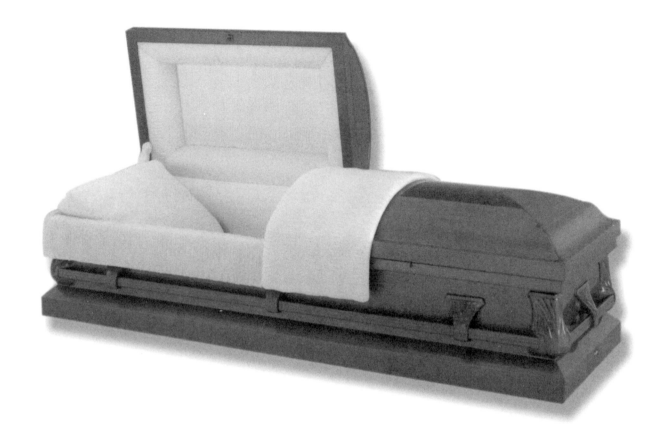

NONPROTECTIVE CASKET
(Metal)

Casket Type
    Half Couch or Perfection-cut (casket lid opens in two pieces)

Exterior Materials
    Steel, 20-gauge

Interior Materials
    Crepe
    Twill

CASKET PICTURES AND DESCRIPTIONS

NONPROTECTIVE CASKET
(Wood)

Casket Type
>   Half Couch or Perfection-cut (casket lid opens in two pieces)

Exterior Materials
>   Mahogany
>   Walnut
>   Cherry Wood
>   Maple
>   Pecan
>   Oak
>   Poplar

Interior Materials
>   Velvet
>   Crepe

NONPROTECTIVE CASKET
(Wood)

Casket Type
      Flat-top Fiberboard (casket lid opens in two pieces)

Exterior Materials
      Softwood Covered with Cloth Material

Interior Materials
      Satin
      Paper

NONPROTECTIVE CASKET
(Wood)

Casket Type
      Orthodox Flat Top

Exterior Materials
      Pine
      Redwood

Interior Materials
      Satin
      Paper

PRICING PRACTICES
Chapter 11

GENERAL PRICE LIST REQUIREMENTS

The general price list must be given to anyone upon request. It is also presented to the next of kin (or representative) prior to any discussion on arrangements. This was part of the Federal Trade Commission Funeral Rule put into place in an effort to create a valid method of price comparison among funeral homes. The Rule requires all items available for purchase to be itemized.

Prior to enacting this Rule, funeral homes generally utilized a unit pricing method with only one price for the services, the casket was then added to the service charge. Consumers used different, or limited, services, yet they were charged the same as if they had used all of the funeral home's services. It was not uncommon to include all of the services in the price of the casket. The more expensive caskets typically included a greater amount of services than an inexpensive casket, which was deemed unfair to the consumer.

It was also standard practice to tell families that embalming was required when there was no public viewing, even when the deceased was to be cremated. Funeral homes are, in fact, allowed to set certain policies such as not allowing public viewing of the deceased without first embalming. The only requirement is that a funeral director is not allowed to charge for embalming without first obtaining permission from the next of kin.

Following is a *sample* price list, indicating the *majority of items* which may be found in the required list of any funeral home in America.

HOMETOWN FUNERAL HOME
123 Main Street
Town, State, 12345

<u>**General Price List**</u>

These prices are effective as of _____ _date_ _____.
They are subject to change without notice.

Value of Trust

Many funeral homes offer a *Value of Trust* statement indicating they have confidence that the service provided will be satisfactory. If, for any reason, the consumer is dissatisfied with a service rendered, a refund will be made regarding the specific service upon written request.

Method of Payment

Most funeral homes require *payment in full* prior to setting the services or viewing times. It is a generally accepted practice to pay the entire bill for merchandise and services at the time of the arrangement conference. Acceptable methods of payment are mostly by cash, check, credit card, verifiable insurance policy assigned, or approved credit from a lending institution. It is generally unacceptable to include funeral products and services in the probate aspect of any estate.

Pricing Methods

Funeral homes are required to provide itemized pricing for all tangible products and services available. They are also allowed to offer Personalized Service Program Packages, however, clearly explaining potential variables or exceptions in writing, such as the following:

> The products and services which follow are those we can provide to our customers. You may choose only the items you desire. However, any funeral arrangements you select will include a charge for our basic services and overhead. If legal or other requirements mean you must buy any items you did not specifically ask for, we will explain the reason, in writing, on the statement we provide describing the funeral products and services you selected.

ITEMIZED SERVICES

BASIC PROFESSIONAL SERVICES OF FUNERAL DIRECTOR AND STAFF $_____

This is the basic charge to each family we serve, offering our professional expertise. It includes, but is not limited to, a proportional share of the taxes, licenses, utilities, and business expenses necessary to service the public in a professional manner. Also included in this charge is the care and shelter of the remains for up to three days; consultation with the family; clerical and administrative services; preparation and filing of necessary permits; consultation with the clergy, cemetery, crematory, or common carrier; planning the funeral or memorial service; and placement of obituary notices. There will be an additional charge for the direction and supervision of each service requested or required.

The fee for basic services and overhead will be added to the total cost of the funeral arrangements selected. This fee is already included in our charges for direct cremation, immediate burial, and receiving or forwarding remains.

EMBALMING $_____

Embalming is a chemical process which provides temporary preservation of the body and eliminates certain health hazards. A person licensed by this state must complete the procedure. Except in some specific cases, embalming is not required by law. Embalming may be necessary, however, if certain funeral arrangements are selected—such as viewing.

If embalming is not chosen, the customer usually has the right to choose an arrangement that eliminates embalming charges, such as in direct cremation or immediate burial. It is the policy of this funeral home to require embalming for any arrangements which include public viewing or visitation.

OTHER CARE OF THE DECEASED

Washing, Bathing, Dressing, Cosmetology, Casketing, etc. $_____

Care and Shelter of Remains for Initial 3-day Period $_____

Care and Shelter *per day* Following Initial 3-day Period $_____

Special Care for Autopsied Remains $_____

USE OF FACILITIES AND STAFF SERVICES

The following charges are those for use of facilities, equipment, vehicles, and/or staff services during normal business hours of 9:00 a.m. through 8:00 p.m., daily, except for New Year's Day, the Fourth of July, Labor Day, Thanksgiving Day, and Christmas Day.

Use of facility for visitation, and services of funeral director and staff in supervising:

Visitation period per day $_____

Additional charge for *each* period of visitation per day $_____

Use of facility for services and/or arrangements under the supervision of funeral director and staff:

In this funeral home's chapel $_____

In a facility other than this funeral home $_____

For a memorial service without the deceased, in this chapel $_____

For a memorial service without the deceased, outside this funeral home $_____

At graveside, cryptside, or other committal location $_____

Committal service for cremated remains or a marker unveiling $_____

AUTOMOTIVE AND TRANSPORT SERVICES

Removal and transfer of remains to funeral home within a 25-mile
radius $_____

Use of funeral coach and driver for transport of remains within a
25-mile radius $_____

Limousine and driver for local transportation services available
to family with a maximum of 4 hours per vehicle $_____

Additional Transport Charges:

Local pickup or delivery of cremated remains $_____

Transfer of remains from the airport $_____

Transport beyond a 25-mile radius, per mile $_____

OTHER PRODUCTS AND SERVICES

Clothing $_____

Acknowledgment cards, per 25 $_____

Memorial Register Book $_____

Memorial folders, per 100 $_____

Prayer cards, per 100 $_____

Memorial paper goods package $_____

Combination shipping container for noncasketed remains $_____

Air tray for casketed remains $_____

Religious items, i.e., a cross, Jewish candle, fraternal emblems, etc. $_____

Alternative cremation container made of cardboard $_____

Packaging and mailing cremated remains $_____

Cremation process fee $_____

CASH ADVANCE ITEMS

Certified copies of Death Certificate, per copy $_____

Recommended clergy honorarium $_____

Recommended organist/musician honorarium $_____

Recommended vocalist honorarium $_____

Newspaper or other obituary notices $_____

BURIAL PRODUCTS

This funeral home offers numerous styles and prices of caskets and alternative containers from which to select. Since many caskets similar in appearance may differ greatly in quality and construction, the following is provided to assist you in making an informed decision.

There are two basic types of caskets.

Wood: Wood caskets are constructed from varying species of hardwood or softwood. Some wood caskets may be covered with cloth. Because wood is a porous material, such caskets are not designed to resist the entrance of air, water, or other outside elements.

Metal: Metal caskets may contain various thicknesses of bronze, copper, stainless steel, or steel. There are many styles and colors to choose from. Most metal caskets are designed to resist the entrance of air, water, and other outside elements.

Warranty Disclaimer: The only warranty of the casket or any merchandise sold in connection with this service is the express written warranty, if any, granted by the manufacturer. This funeral home makes no warranty, expressed or implied, including an implied warranty of suitability or fitness for a particular purpose, with respect to the casket and/or outer burial container.

PRODUCTS

Casket Prices Range from $_____ to $_____
    A complete price list is provided at the funeral home,
    including prices for burial and cremation-designed caskets.

Outer Burial Prices Range from $_____ to $_____
    A complete list is available at the funeral home.

Urn Prices Range from $_____ to $_____
    A complete list is available at the funeral home.

Alternative Container Prices Range from $_____ to $_____
    A complete list is available at the funeral home.

PERSONALIZED SERVICE PROGRAM PACKAGES

Most families select a personalized service program package. The following list of specifically composed "packages" may help you to select the desired arrangements. Only the items listed are included with the packages.

If additional products or services are desired to further personalize the package, such items may be selected from the items shown under OTHER PRODUCTS AND SERVICES (in pages previous to this).

TRADITIONAL FUNERAL HOME CHAPEL OR CHURCH SERVICE WITH VISITATION

Personalized package includes:
> Basic professional services of funeral director and staff;
> Embalming and other care of the deceased to include washing, bathing, dressing, cosmetology, casketing, etc.;
> Use of facility for visitation and services of funeral director and staff in supervising visitation periods;
> Use of funeral home, other place of worship, or other facility, and services of funeral director and staff in supervising service;
> Use of equipment and services of staff for graveside, cryptside, or other committal location;
> Automotive equipment to include removal and transfer of the remains to funeral home, within a 25-mile radius;
> Funeral coach and driver for local transport; and
> Convenience package of memorial paper goods.

This personalized package <u>does not</u> include:
> Products selected such as a casket, outer burial container; or
> Any cash advance items.

Total Traditional Funeral Home Chapel or Church Service with Visitation $_____

TRADITIONAL GRAVESIDE SERVICE WITH VISITATION

Personalized package includes:
> Basic professional services of funeral director and staff;
> Embalming, and other care of the deceased to include washing, bathing, dressing, cosmetology, casketing, etc.;
> Use of facility for visitation and services of funeral director and staff in supervising visitation periods;

Use of equipment and services of staff for graveside, cryptside, or other committal location;

Automotive equipment to include removal and transfer of the remains to funeral home, within a 25-mile radius;

Funeral coach and driver for local transport; and

Convenience package of memorial paper goods.

This personalized package does not include:

Products selected such as a casket, outer burial container; or

Any cash advance items.

Total Traditional Graveside Service with Visitation $_____

TRADITIONAL CREMATION "SERVICE" IN FUNERAL HOME OR PLACE OF WORSHIP

Personalized package includes:

Basic professional services of funeral director and staff;

Embalming, and other care of the deceased to include washing, bathing, dressing, cosmetology, casketing, etc.;

Use of facility for visitation and services of funeral director and staff in supervising visitation periods;

Use of funeral home, other place of worship, or other facility, and services of funeral director and staff in supervising service;

Automotive equipment to include removal and transfer of the remains to funeral home, within a 25-mile radius;

Funeral coach and driver for local transport;

A convenience package of memorial paper goods; and

Cremation process fee.

This personalized package does not include:

Products selected such as a casket or an urn for the cremains; or

Any cash advace items.

Total Traditional Cremation Service in Funeral Home or Place of Worship $_____

Cremation Products:

Caskets designed for Cremation range from $_____ to $_____

Urns range from $_____ to $_____

Total Traditional Cremation Service with Rental Casket $_____

SERVICE OF REMEMBRANCE WITH DIRECT CREMATION

Personalized package includes:

A proportionate share of basic professional services of funeral director and staff;

Use of facility, other place of worship, or other facility without the deceased present; and services of funeral director and staff in supervising service;

Automotive equipment to include removal and transfer of the remains to funeral home, within a 25-mile radius;

Convenience package of memorial paper goods; and

Cremation process fee.

This personalized package <u>does not</u> include:

Embalming or other care of the deceased;

Use of funeral home for visitation and services of funeral director and staff in supervising visitation periods;

Products selected such as a cremation casket or an urn for the cremains; or

Any cash advance items.

Total Service of Remembrance with Direct Cremation $

Total Service of Remembrance with Cardboard Container $_____

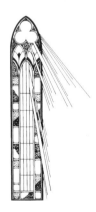

OTHER PERSONALIZED SERVICES

GRAVESIDE SERVICE WITH FAMILY VISITATION ONLY

Personalized package includes:

Basic professional services of funeral director and staff;

Embalming, and other care of the deceased to include washing, bathing, dressing, cosmetology, casketing, etc.;

Use of the facility for two hours of private family visitation;

Use of equipment and services of funeral director and staff in supervising service at graveside, cryptside, or other committal location;

Automotive equipment to include removal and transfer of the remains to funeral home, within a 25-mile radius;

Funeral coach and driver for local transport; and

Convenience package of memorial paper goods.

This personalized package does not include:

Use of funeral home, other place of worship, or other facility for service;

Products selected such as a casket, outer burial container; or

Any cash advance items.

Total Graveside Services with Family Visitation $_____

MINIMUM GRAVESIDE SERVICE WITH NO VISITATION

Personalized package includes:

Basic professional services of funeral director and staff;

Other care of the deceased to include washing, bathing, dressing, cosmetology, and casketing, etc.;

Use of equipment and services of funeral director and staff in supervising service at graveside, cryptside, or other committal location;

Automotive equipment to include removal and transfer of the remains to funeral home, within a 25-mile radius;

Funeral coach and driver for local transport; and

Convenience package of memorial paper goods.

This personalized package does not include:

Embalming or other care of the deceased;

Use of facility for visitation, funeral, or memorial service;

Products selected such as a casket, outer burial container; or

Any cash advance items.

Total Minimum Graveside Service with No Visitation $_____

MINIMUM SERVICE OPTIONS

DIRECT CREMATION WITHOUT VISITATION OR SERVICE

This personalized package includes:
>A proportionate share of basic professional services of funeral director and staff;
>Automotive equipment to include removal and transfer of the remains to funeral home, within a 25-mile radius; and
>Cremation process fee.

This personalized package does not include:
>Embalming or other care of the deceased;
>Use of facility for visitation, funeral, or memorial service;
>Products selected such as an urn for the cremains or convenience package of memorial paper goods; or
>Any cash advance items

Note: The cremation container used by the funeral home is made of cardboard.

Direct Cremation with Container Provided by Family $_____

Direct Cremation with Cardboard Container $_____

Direct Cremation with Casket ranging from $_____ to $_____

IMMEDIATE BURIAL WITHOUT VISITATION OR SERVICE

This personalized package includes:
>A proportionate share of basic professional services of funeral director and staff;
>Automotive equipment to include removal and transfer of the remains to funeral home, within a 25-mile radius; and
>Funeral coach and driver for local transport.

This personalized package does not include:
>Embalming or other care of the deceased;
>Use of facility for visitation, funeral, or memorial service;
>Products selected such as a casket, outer burial container, convenience package of memorial paper goods; or
>Any cash advance items.

Total Immediate Burial with Casket by Family $_____

Total Immediate Burial with Casket ranging from $_____ to $_____

FORWARDING REMAINS TO ANOTHER FUNERAL HOME WITHOUT VISITATION OR SERVICES

Personalized package includes:
>A proportionate share of basic professional services of funeral director and staff;
>Embalming;
>Automotive equipment to include removal and transfer of the remains to funeral home, within a 25-mile radius; and transfer to airport.

This personalized package <u>does not</u> include:
>Washing, bathing, dressing, cosmetology, and casketing, etc.;
>Use of facility for visitation, funeral, or memorial service;
>Other funeral home or transport charges;
>Products selected such as a casket or convenience package of memorial paper goods; or
>Any cash advance items.

Total Forwarding of Remains to Another Funeral Home, Etc. $_____

RECEIVING REMAINS FROM ANOTHER FUNERAL HOME

Personalized package includes:
>A proportionate share of basic professional services of funeral director and staff; and
>Transport from the airport to the funeral home.

This personalized package <u>does not</u> include:
>Embalming or other care of the deceased;
>Use of facility for visitation, funeral, or memorial service;
>Convenience package of memorial paper goods; or
>Any cash advance items.

Total Receiving of Remains from Another Funeral Home $_____

CASKET PRICE LIST REQUIREMENTS

This price list must be made available to anyone upon request. Further, it must be presented to the next of kin (or representative) prior to discussing any casket selection. This was part of the Federal Trade Commission Funeral Rule put into place in an effort to create a true method of price comparison among funeral homes. The Rule requires that all caskets available for sale must be listed on the price list, which includes a description of both exterior and interior materials used in their construction.

The majority of the items contained in the following sample Casket Price List should be found in any funeral home in the United States.

HOMETOWN FUNERAL HOME
123 Main Street
Town, State, 12345

CASKET PRICE LIST

**These prices are effective as of _____ _date_____.
They are subject to change without notice.**

The funeral home makes no representation or warranty regarding caskets. The only warranties granted in connection with goods sold by this funeral service, whether expressed or implied, are the written warranties, if any, extended by the manufacturers thereof. No other warranties and, specifically, no implied warranties of suitability and/or fitness for a particular purpose are extended by the seller.

UNIT #	NAME	EXTERIOR	INTERIOR	PRICE
		Bronze		
1	President	48-oz Solid Bronze	Velvet	_____
2	Regent	32-oz Solid Bronze	Velvet	_____
		Copper		
3	Diplomat	48-oz Solid Copper	Velvet	_____
4	Queen	32-oz Solid Copper	Velvet	_____
		Steel		
5	Regal	Stainless Steel Brushed	Velvet	_____
6	Tiger	16-gauge Steel	Velvet	_____
7	Gold Leaf	18-gauge Steel	Velvet	_____
8	Midnight	18-gauge Steel	Crepe	_____
9	Victory	20-gauge Steel	Crepe	_____
10	King	20-gauge Steel	Crepe	_____
		Wood		
11	State	Solid Maple	Crepe	_____
12	Harmony	Solid Oak	Crepe	_____
13	Tranquility	Solid Poplar	Crepe	_____
		Speciality Caskets		
14	Polished	Solid Oak - Orthodox	Crepe	_____
15	Unfinished	Solid Poplar - Orthodox	Twill	_____
16	Oversize	20-gauge Steel	Crepe	_____
		Rental Casket		
17	Rental	Solid Oak - with Insert	Crepe	_____
		Alternative Container		
18	Cremation	Cardboard Container	None	_____

SAMPLES OF NECESSARY FORMS
Chapter 12

FORMS

Because forms to be completed by you throughout this publication are limited to one of each, it is suggested that the user have copies made of any of those forms (s)he intends to use.

The reasons are twofold:

1)   Errors (spelling, names, filling in a the wrong blank with incorrect answers, etc.) may easily be made on any form, and it would become difficult, if not impossible, to erase, depending on use of typewriter or pen, rather than pencil; and

2)   Within a family unit, more than one person might have need/use of the form.

While you have the option to tear pages out of the book, a good copy shop can reproduce them on a machine without tearing out the pages.

Please Note: **The author grants permission for the reader to reproduce, for his or her personal use only but not for any commercial use, the above referred to forms. The contents of this book are copyrighted, and no violations of copyright laws will be tolerated, with exception to the above-granted permission.**

CORONER/MEDICAL EXAMINER RELEASE

There is often confusion about the role of a coroner or medical examiner. Always dependent upon each state's mandates, the *American Heritage Dictionary* defines a coroner as "A public officer [who may or may not be a physician] whose primary function is to investigate by inquest any death thought to be of other than natural causes." A medical examiner is defined as "A physician officially authorized by a governmental unit (as a city or county) to ascertain causes of death, esp. those not occurring under natural circumstances." Both are extensions of the police department.

The coroner/medical examiner determines if an autopsy is necessary, based on:
    (a) if there is no absolutely apparent reason for the death;
    (b) if there is no physician willing to sign the death certificate as to the cause of death;
    (c) if the death is due to any type of force or traumatic cause, *when an autopsy will usually be performed.*

Once an autopsy or medical examination is completed, the coroner/medical examiner's office will call and release the deceased to the funeral home. Note that the coroner/medical examiner requires that a form be signed by the next of kin (representative) authorizing their office's release of the deceased to the funeral home the next of kin has selected.

Each local or state government has specific rules or laws as to when the coroner/medical examiner's office must be notified of a death. No one outside of the law enforcement community is consulted in this matter. If the coroner/medical examiner's office determines that an autopsy will be performed, next of kin has no right to overrule such a decision. Nor may next of kin determine if such autopsy should be performed. That duty rests solely with the coroner/medical examiner.

You should note that a Coroner/Medical Examiner's *Authorization for Release of Remains* must be signed by both the next of kin and the funeral home (or their designated representatives). Only after that form is completed by the next of kin (representative) will the coroner/medical examiner's office notify the named funeral home and release the deceased to them.

Following is a <u>sample</u> *Authorization for Release of Remains* form:

Coroner/Medical Examiner's Name
(Complete Address)

AUTHORIZATION FOR RELEASE OF REMAINS

Name of Deceased_____

I/we, the legal next of kin (or designated representative), do hereby authorize and direct the Coroner/Medical Examiner of (*name of jurisdiction*) to release the remains of the aforementioned decedent to:

Name of Funeral Home_____

The undersigned assumes any liability which might fall upon the office of the Coroner/Medical Examiner of (*jurisdiction*) for the release of the aforementioned decedent, as directed by the next of kin (or representative).

Date_____   **Signature**_____

Relationship_____   **Witness**_____

RECEIPT FOR REMAINS:

On this date, (___*date*___) I received from the office of the Coroner/Medical Examiner of (*jurisdiction*) the remains of the aforementioned decedent.

Signature_____

Funeral Home Name_____

PERMISSION FOR AUTOPSY

A coroner/medical examiner is not involved in a death if the decedent is under the care of a physician (at the time of death) who determines that cause of death was not due to any force or trauma. It is not unusual, however, for an attending physician to ask the next of kin to grant permission to perform an autopsy. This is especially true if the death occurs in a hospital with a medical school.

An autopsy is the surgical procedure to examine internal organs to more conclusively determine cause of death. For an autopsy to be done by a hospital pathology department, or by an independent pathologist, an *Authorization for Autopsy* form must be signed.

The pathologist will want to know in advance what is to be achieved by the procedure. If the primary purpose is to gather evidence for suspected malpractice by a hospital or attending physician, it might be difficult to convince a pathologist to perform the procedure. Most are not interested in getting involved in autopsies which require them to go to court as expert witnesses against a hospital or another physician.

Following is a <u>sample</u> of an *Authorization for Autopsy* form which must be signed by the next of kin prior to an autopsy being scheduled.

Name of Physician
(Complete Address)

AUTHORIZATION FOR AUTOPSY

I, _____, bearing the relationship

Name of Person Requesting Autopsy

of _____ to _____, hereby authorize a

Spouse or Other Next of Kin　　　　　　　Name of Deceased

complete autopsy on the body of _____, and obtaining and

Name of Deceased

preserving the tissues and fluids necessary for diagnosis.

I hold _____ and his/her associates free of any liability in

Name of Physician

the performance of this autopsy.

Signature_____

Spouse or Other Next of Kin

Signature_____

Witness

Date Signed_____

PERMISSION TO EMBALM

The Federal Trade Commission passed the "Funeral Trade Rule" which requires funeral homes to obtain permission from the next of kin to embalm.

There are few instances in which a body *must* be embalmed. One example is the necessity to transport the deceased across state lines or on a commercial carrier—if death occurs away from the place of final disposition.

Following is an example of an *Authorization to Embalm* form to be signed by the next of kin prior to embalming. Verbal permission may be obtained, initially, followed by written permission when completing the funeral arrangements.

AUTHORIZATION TO EMBALM

The undersigned hereby authorizes_____

Name of Funeral Home

and/or its agents to care for, embalm, and otherwise prepare for burial and other

disposition, the remains of_____

Name of Deceased

I/we hereby represent that I am/we are of the same and nearest degree of relationship to the deceased, and legally authorized or charged with the responsibility for such burial and/or other disposition.

_____   _____

Name - Printed   Relationship to Deceased

_____

Signature

_____   _____

Name - Printed   Relationship to Deceased

_____

Signature

_____   _____

Witness   Date

CERTIFICATE OF DEATH

The Death Certificate is a legal document which must be completed by the funeral home, then filed with the health district in the city or state's vital statistics office.

It is necessary that the documented information be correct as it may be used for *(a)* transfer of property; *(b)* probating the estate; *(c)* collecting life insurance or other benefits; or *(d)* changing bank accounts. If any incorrect data is given to the funeral home, or if the funeral home errs in filling out the form, an "Affidavit of Change" must be submitted in order to correct the original certificate.

Once completed by the funeral home, the death certificate is taken to the attending physician or the office of the coroner/medical examiner for signature and cause of death certification. After the necessary signature is obtained, the original death certificate is filed with the city/state's vital statistics office. A clerk will check the death certificate to ascertain that cause of death is properly noted, that it is completed in full, and that there are no errors. When the clerk has signed and dated the death certificate, (s)he will issue a "Disposition Permit," and produce the requested number of certified copies. A disposition permit must be obtained prior to burial, out-of-state transport, or cremation.

Following is a typical list of questions to be answered by the next of kin to complete the certificate required and a sample copy of a death certificate form.

INFORMATION NEEDED TO COMPLETE THE CERTIFICATE OF DEATH FORM

First, middle, and last name of decedent

Date of death, month, day, and year

County of death

City, town, or location of death

Hospital/Institution name, or address where death occurred

Age, month, day, and year of birth

State/country of birth

Citizen of what country

Highest educational level

Marital status at time of death

First, middle, and/or maiden name of spouse

Social Security Number

Primary occupation during majority of life/kind of business or industry

Street address, city, county, and state of residence of Decedent

Father's first, middle, and last name

Father's state/country of birth

Mother's first, middle, and maiden name

Mother's state/country of birth

First, middle, and last name of person supplying the information

Relationship of informant to Decedent

Street address, city, county, and state of residence of informant

Disposition: burial, cremation, or removal out of state

Name, street address, city, county, and state of cemetery or crematory

Name, street address, city, county, and state of funeral home

Note: The balance of information will be completed by the attending physician or the coroner/medical examiner.

CERTIFICATE OF DEATH

LOCAL FILE NUMBER

STATE FILE NUMBER

TYPE
R PRINT
IN
RMANENT
ACK INK

DECEASED—NAME First Middle Last	DATE OF DEATH (Month, Day, Year)	COUNTY OF DEATH
1.	2.	3a.

CITY, TOWN OR LOCATION OF DEATH	HOSPITAL OR OTHER INSTITUTION—Name (If not either, give street and number)	If Hosp. or Inst. indicate DOA, OP/Emer. Rm. Inpatient (Specify)	SEX
3b.	3c.	3e.	4.

CEDENT

RACE—(e.g., White, Black, American Indian, etc.) (Specify)	Was Decedent of Hispanic Origin? Specify ☐ yes ☐ no If yes, specify Mexican, Cuban, Puerto Rican, etc.	AGE—Last Birthday (Years)	UNDER 1 YEAR MOS : DAYS	UNDER 1 DAY HOURS : MINS	DATE OF BIRTH (Mo., Day, Yr.)
5.	6.	7a.	7b.	7c.	8.

IF DEATH
CCURRED IN
STITUTION
E HANDBOOK
EGARDING
MPLETION OF
IDENCE ITEMS

STATE OF BIRTH (If not U.S.A., name country)	CITIZEN OF WHAT COUNTRY	Decedent's Education. Specify highest grade completed.	MARRIED, NEVER MARRIED, WIDOWED, DIVORCED (Specify)	SURVIVING SPOUSE (If wife, give maiden name)
9a.	9b.	10.	11.	12.

SOCIAL SECURITY NUMBER	USUAL OCCUPATION (Give Kind of Work Done During Most of Working Life, Even If Retired)	KIND OF BUSINESS OR INDUSTRY
13.	14a.	14b.

RESIDENCE—STATE	COUNTY	CITY, TOWN, OR LOCATION	STREET AND NUMBER	INSIDE CITY LIMITS (Specify Yes or No)
15a.	15b.	15c.	15d.	15e.

RENTS

FATHER—NAME First Middle Last	MOTHER—MAIDEN NAME First Middle Last
16.	17.

INFORMANT—NAME (Type or Print)	MAILING ADDRESS (Street or R.F.D. No., City or Town, State, Zip)
18a.	18b.

BURIAL, CREMATION, REMOVAL, OTHER (Specify)	CEMETERY OR CREMATORY—NAME	LOCATION City or Town State
19a.	19b.	19c.

POSITION

FUNERAL DIRECTOR—SIGNATURE (Or Person Acting as Such)	FUNERAL DIRECTOR LICENSE NUMBER	NAME AND ADDRESS OF FACILITY
20a. ▶	20b.	20c.

RTIFIER

	To be Completed by CERTIFYING PHYSICIAN	21a. To the best of my knowledge, death occurred at the time, date and place and due to the cause(s) stated.		To be completed by Coroner's Office	22a. On the basis of examination and/or investigation, in my opinion death occurred at the time, date and place and due to the cause(s) and manner stated.

21a. (Signature and Title) ▶

22a. (Signature and Title) ▶

DATE SIGNED (Mo., Day, Yr.)	HOUR OF DEATH	DATE SIGNED (Mo., Day, Yr.)	HOUR OF DEATH
21b.	21c.	22b.	22c.

NAME OF ATTENDING PHYSICIAN IF OTHER THAN CERTIFIER (Type or Print)	PRONOUNCED DEAD (Mo., Day, Yr.)	PRONOUNCED DEAD (Hour)
21d.	22d. ON	22e. AT

NAME AND ADDRESS OF CERTIFIER (PHYSICIAN, ATTENDING PHYSICIAN, MEDICAL EXAMINER, OR CORONER). (Type or Print.)	LICENSE NUMBER
23a.	23b.

REGISTRAR	DATE RECEIVED BY REGISTRAR (Mo., Day, Yr.)	DEATH DUE TO COMMUNICABLE DISEASE
24a. (Signature) ▶	24b.	24c. YES ☐ NO ☐

NDITIONS
IF ANY
ICH GAVE
RISE TO
MEDIATE
CAUSE
ATING THE
DERLYING
USE LAST

25. IMMEDIATE CAUSE (ENTER ONLY ONE CAUSE PER LINE FOR (a), (b), AND (c).)	Interval between onset and death
PART I (a)	
DUE TO, OR AS A CONSEQUENCE OF:	Interval between onset and death
(b)	
DUE TO, OR AS A CONSEQUENCE OF:	Interval between onset and death
(c)	

USE OF
DEATH

PART II	OTHER SIGNIFICANT CONDITIONS—Conditions contributing to death but not resulting in the underlying cause given in Part 1.	AUTOPSY (Specify Yes or No) 26.	WAS CASE REFERRED TO CORONER (Specify Yes or No) 27.

ACC., SUICIDE, HOM., UNDET., OR PENDING INVEST. (Specify) 28a.	DATE OF INJURY (Mo., Day, Yr.) 28b.	HOUR OF INJURY 28c. M	DESCRIBE HOW INJURY OCCURRED 28d.

INJURY AT WORK (Specify Yes or No) 28e.	PLACE OF INJURY—At home, farm, street, factory, office building, etc. (Specify) 28f.	LOCATION. STREET OR R.F.D. No. CITY OR TOWN STATE 28g.

105

PERSONAL PROPERTY RELEASE AND INDEMNITY

Most funeral homes require that a release of liability and indemnification agreement be signed by the next of kin (representative) if jewelry or other valuables are left with the funeral director to be placed with or on the deceased in the casket. Leaving such valuables places a burden on the funeral home relative to security; consequently, most will not accept this responsibility without a release.

Families must clearly explain which items are to be buried or cremated with the deceased, and which are to be returned. It is also imperative to inform the funeral home exactly who these valuables are to be returned to. Due to the emotional state at the time of a service, it is easy for someone grieving to misplace items of importance. Extra care must be taken when retrieving such items from the funeral home.

Following is an example of a *Release & Indemnity Regarding Personal Property* form that funeral homes may require next of kin (representative) to sign if anything other than clothing is to be left in the care of the funeral director.

HOMETOWN FUNERAL HOME
123 Main Street
Town, State, 12345

RELEASE & INDEMNITY REGARDING
PERSONAL PROPERTY

The undersigned delivered items to our funeral home, requesting that they be placed on or with the remains of:

_____
Name of Decedent

during the period between death, burial/entombment, cremation, or other agreed disposition, namely:

1. _____   4. _____

2. _____   5. _____

3. _____   6. _____

The undersigned represents that (s)he has the right to make such delivery and request, and assumes all responsibility for damage or loss including, but not limited to, third-party theft, of any and all such items during the entire period while this funeral home has custody of the decedent's body.

The undersigned further requests burial/entombment, or cremation with the deceased, each/all item(s) encircled and initialed here:

1._____ 2._____ 3._____ 4._____ 5._____ 6._____

The undersigned requests this funeral home to return to undersigned, after completion of services, item(s):

1._____ 2._____ 3._____ 4._____ 5._____ 6._____

The undersigned represents that (s)he/they has/have full rights and authority to act as set forth above, and hereby indemnify and agree to defend our firm against any or all claims, which might be made by any person against this firm, by virtue of any of the items or actions described hereinabove.

Signature_____   Relationship_____

Signature_____   Relationship_____

Witness_____   Date_____

MEMORIAL MARKERS/HEADSTONES
Chapter 13

MEMORIAL MARKERS

Most cemeteries have specific rules as to the composition and placement of markers.

Older and/or historical cemeteries accepted upright or flat "headstones" with little or no uniformity in style, size, or design. Today's cemeteries are mostly "endowment care memorial parks," meaning that a one-time fee is charged at the time of interment, entombment, or inurnment to perpetually maintain the grave and cemetery. For this reason, many are restricted to use of flat markers (floral vases are usually part of the marker design).

With the increasing popularity of cremation, there are now options for the placement of cremated remains. The markers may be either single or double in design—the double indicating the cremains of two within the same site.

The following pictures show the types of markers most used today. They are made of granite, bronze, or bronze on a granite base.

Bronze Marker on Granite Base

Pictured in double-design to cover two graves

Available with or without a floral vase

Also available in single-design to cover one grave

Available with or without a floral vase

Single Granite Marker

Pictured in single-design to cover one grave
Also available in double-design to cover two graves

Designed without a floral vase
(vase is often placed above marker)

Bronze Cremorial Marker on Granite Base

Pictured in double-design to include two cremated remains
Also available in single-design to include one cremated remains

Available with or without a floral vase

URNS AND THEIR USAGE
Chapter 14

ABOUT URNS

Only in the 14th Century did the term "Urn" appear, in the writings of English poet Chaucer, then defined as a footed or pedestaled vessel in which to preserve the ashes of the dead. They were used for the same purpose in Ancient Greece millennia before the English word came into use. Urns were fashioned from materials available in their own time and place.

Although cremation dates back to the ancients, practiced among most societies, it has only recently become a more accepted choice in the United States and Canada. Various religious faiths have different laws governing cremation. For instance, Roman Catholics now permit it, but only after two millennia and as the result of their 2nd Ecumenical Council in the late 1960s. Religious leaders of most denominations are available in virtually every town and city to advise of any cremation laws or restrictions.

Urn Usage
It should be kept in mind that many individuals and families selecting the dispersion of cremains later regret the decision. Once they are gone, there is no permanent place to later visit and reflect, particularly on holidays or anniversaries. For this reason, careful consideration should be given to permanent placement and memorialization of cremated remains, particularly within an urn.

Although cremains may be scattered over land or water, be aware that every community has laws and restrictions which either allow or prohibit such scattering. Any funeral director can advise you of such local ordinances.

Urn Placement
While some may choose to have their cremains spread, when the decision is left to next of kin, they more often prefer placing the deceased's cremains into an urn, whether to be buried in a family's cemetery plot, placed in a niche at a columbarium, or kept in the home.

Selecting an Urn
Deciding what is to be done with cremated remains will help in deciding what kind of urn, if any, is right for a departed loved one. Choosing an urn is very important since it provides both a protective and dignified receptacle for a loved one's cremains. It can be made the focal point at a memorial service, and/or serve as a permanent commemorative for the deceased.

Urns are crafted from various materials: cast bronze, marble, wood, or sheet bronze. Their widely ranged prices are based on materials used and design details. For example, an urn can be personalized with phrases or special verses, emblems—even pictures of the deceased.

A few of the options available when selecting an urn follow.

Classic Marble Urn

Cast Bronze Urn

Cast Sheet Urn

Mohagany Hardwood Urn

Cherry Hardwood Urn

Hardwood Urn Cabinet

PREARRANGING
Chapter 15

THE NEED FOR PREARRANGEMENTS

Benjamin Franklin told us that "In this world nothing is certain but death and taxes." Although science causes us to live longer today than ever before, death remains the conclusion to life.

Realizing the reality of the eventual end of life, it is important, and extremely helpful, to be prepared for a final service and disposition arrangements. Prearranging funerals, memorial services, or remains disposition tends to take a back seat to all other responsibilities in life. We constantly outline and predetermine our daily activities, vacations, estates, etc. Yet, most of us fail to remember what is perhaps the most important plan of all: the one to help our loved ones better cope with that inevitable day.

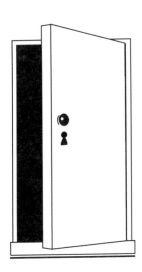

INFORMATION VS CONTRACT

Information Only

Prearranging a funeral, memorial service, or final disposition can be as simple as letting our family members know what our wishes are in the event that we die unexpectedly. Important information can be verbally communicated to our families, or written and placed in a convenient location so that our wishes may be carried out. There is always great confusion within a family when a loved one has died, which proper preplanning can lighten. Some funeral homes will allow information to be completed and kept on file without a formal contract or financial commitment.

Contract

It is possible to contract with a funeral home and cemetery for final arrangements in advance. There are several options for payment; however, each state has its own regulations and laws regarding prepaid contracts. A traditional funeral service and burial can be expensive. By prearranging and prepaying for this eventual need, financial burden can be avoided and some emotional pain may be diminished for the spouse or family when death occurs.

Trust Contracts

Many states allow funeral homes and cemeteries to sell prearranged merchandise and services with money placed into a trust at a bank or other acceptable financial institution. Trust laws differ from state-to-state as to how much money must be placed in trust. If prepaid items are delivered to the consumer, such as a space in a cemetery, it is then unnecessary to place the money into a trust account. This is, of course, after payment has been made to the cemetery for the space and the deed has been delivered.

Some states permit a portion of the money paid to be used for commissions and administrative expenses. After these amounts have been paid, the balance is placed in trust until the contract has been fulfilled at some future date. A few states allow contracts as long as one hundred percent of the money is placed into a trust.

A wide variety of rules dictate how the interest is treated. Depending on each state's statutes, the interest may belong entirely to the funeral home or cemetery, or to the purchaser of the contract. Laws also vary as to how much money will be returned to the contract purchaser in the event of a cancellation. When prearranging using a trust, it is imperative to know the laws of the state where the contract is purchased.

Insurance Contracts

The practice of using an insurance policy specifically designed to pay for funeral and cemetery products and services describes the most common prepaid contract.

 The advantage of an insurance contract is that it may be more portable than a trust contract. This means that if you move to a city or state and use a different funeral home/cemetery than originally planned, no significant changes to the insurance contract are needed.

The disadvantage of an insurance-funded contract is that the costs of products and services are not frozen, i.e., if a long period has passed and prices are higher than at the time of entering into the agreement, the increased prices are not covered.

EMOTIONAL VS RATIONAL

Emotional Decisions

If death occurs prior to making choices, the decisions made by loved ones may be based solely on emotions. Families are typically in a period of deep sorrow when they decide on funeral and final disposition arrangements, which they often later regret. While it can be uncomfortable for someone to discuss these matters prior to the death of a loved one, it is much more difficult to do so during the stressful time following a death. Families tend to spend much more money while grieving than during the usually calmer time of preplanning.

Rational Consideration

When prearranging, you are protected against last minute decisions or commitments made without reason or normal caution. The benefit of preplanning is that each preference may be thought through with reason and based on true feelings, not emotional or irrational reactions. Another advantage is that such decisions are based on genuine desires rather than what may be interpreted as needs, under stress. Situations such as these are better analyzed with sufficient time to think, prepare, and act.

FAMILY PORTFOLIO

Recorded Information

Once all prearrangements are complete, it is important to notify the next of kin as to what your desires genuinely are and the arrangements made. Recording all of the information will be very helpful when the time comes to arrange final services and disposition, as well as resolve estate needs.

A note, such as follows, and complete information should be made available to chosen family members or a legal representative, so that your final wishes are known and fulfilled.

SAMPLE LETTER

To my loved ones:

Wishing to spare my loved ones any unnecessary anxiety, expense, and inconvenience at the time of my death, I have recorded the data following, which represents arrangements I have made.

Certain vital statistics and a list of documents which may be needed are recorded in the following pages.

I sincerely hope you will find these arrangements as pleasing to you as they are to me, and that they help to retain a warm memory of the wonderful years we have spent together.

May God bless you all,

Signature:_____

(Spouse's signature):_____

Witness:_____

Date:_____

VITAL STATISTICS AND HISTORICAL DATA

Name:_____
          First   Middle   Last   (Maiden)

Address:_____

City:_____ State:_____ Zip:_____ Phone No.:_____

Birthplace:_____
          City   State or County

Social Security Number:_____ Birth Date:_____

Primary Lifetime Occupation (or retired from):_____

_____

Type of Business:_____

Highest Level of Education Attained:_____

Single_____ Married_____ Widowed_____ Divorced_____

Spouse (if wife, enter maiden name):_____
               First   Middle   Last or Maiden

Name of Father:_____
          First   Middle   Last

Father's Birthplace:_____
          City   State or Country

Name of Mother:_____
          First   Middle   Last   (Maiden)

Mother's Birthplace:_____
          City   State or Country

VETERAN INFORMATION

Name of War(s) or Conflict(s) Served In:_____

_____

Branch of Service:_____Rank:_____

Date Enlisted:_____Where:_____

Date Discharged:_____Where:_____

Service Number:_____"C" Number:_____

Location of Discharge Papers:_____

_____

FUNERAL OR MEMORIAL SERVICE INSTRUCTIONS

Religious Preference (if any):_____

Clergy (if specific choice):_____

Services to be held at: Funeral Home___Church___Other Facility__Graveside__

Lodge Service by:_____

Pallbearers: Selected by Me_____

_____

To be selected by Family____To be selected by Funeral Home_____

Flower Preference(s):_____

Music: Selected by Family_____Selected by Funeral Home_____; and/or my

Specific Selections: 1._____

                       2._____

                       3._____

                       4._____

Clothing:_____

Jewelry:_____

Glasses:_____

Cosmetics:_____

Hair Instructions:_____

Type of Casket Desired:_____

Other Service Instructions:_____

FINAL DISPOSITION PROPERTY INFORMATION

I do have a deed to Cemetery Property

Name of Cemetery:_____

Location of Cemetery:_____
                                  City   State

Cemetery Property in Name of:_____

Name of Mausoleum or Garden:_____

Section:_____ Lot:_____ Block:_____ Plot:_____

Crypt:_____ Niche:_____ Tier:_____

I do not have a deed to Cemetery Property, but would prefer:

Interment:_____ Entombment:_____ Cremation:_____

Please Ship me to:_____
                              City   State

Receiving Funeral Director:_____

FAMILY NOTIFICATION LIST

For assistance to family, please immediately notify the following in order indicated:

Name	Address	Phone #
1		
2		
3		
4		
5		
6		

CLOSE FRIEND AND NEIGHBOR NOTIFICATION LIST

For assistance to family, please immediately notify the following in order indicated:

Name	Address	Phone #
1		
2		
3		
4		
5		
6		

RELATIVES

Name	City & State of Residence
Husband/Wife	
Children	
Parents	
Brothers	
Sisters	

Number of Grandchildren:_____

Number of Great-grandchildren:_____

OBITUARY INFORMATION FOR PUBLICATION

Newspapers and Organizations to be Notified:

1._____

2._____

3._____

4._____

Present/Past Occupation & Position:_____

Name of Firm:_____ from _____ to _____

Came to City & State of :_____ in _____

Previous Residence in City/State/Country of:_____

Schools Attended:_____

Degrees, etc.:_____

Public Office(s) Held:_____

Military Record (Include Citations):_____

_____

Clubs/Civic Organizations:_____

Lodge Affiliations:_____

Additional Information:_____

_____

_____

REGARDING ESTATE INFORMATION

(This information is confidential and very important in the event of a common disaster)

I have_____have not_____made a will/trust. If a will/trust is made, the Executor/Trustee is:

_____
Name   Address   Phone #

A copy is kept at:_____

My attorney is:_____

My bank is:_____ Branch:_____

Safety Deposit Box in:_____

Box Number:_____Location of Key:_____

Real Estate Owned:_____

_____

Location of Deeds:_____

My Insurance Agent is:_____

My Investment Broker is:_____

Notify following Insurance Companies, Unions, Lodges, etc., paying Death Benefits:

1._____   4._____

2._____   5._____

3._____   6._____

Location of Insurance Policies:_____

Additional Information:_____

_____

RELEASE OF REMAINS

To Whom it May Concern (Authorized Authorities, Coroner, Hospital Authority, Funeral Home):

In the event of my death, it is my will and request that_____
Funeral Home

of_____be notified so that they may execute
         City   State

and perform the arrangements contained in this Family Portfolio.

Signed:_____Date:_____

OTHER SPECIAL INFORMATION, REQUESTS, AND/OR REMARKS

ESTATE PRESERVATION ISSUES
Chapter 16

ESTATE ISSUES AND DEATH

How a person holds title to assets (s)he owns is important in determining what is done with his/her estate at death. The estate is also affected by what planning has been done with respect to wills, trusts, family partnerships, insurance trusts, and various other preparational techniques.

The size of the estate is significant, too. In addition to federal laws that have a direct impact on the estate of the deceased, there are many states which impose a state death tax. With proper planning an estate may save literally hundreds of thousands of dollars. It is important to work with an attorney specializing in estate-planning issues to be certain that your estate is protected against the burden of taxation upon death.

Following is an overview of the planning process, and what may be expected by not properly planning prior to death.

Intestacy
A person who dies without a *will* dies "intestate," meaning that his/her property is distributed according to the (*declared* residency*) state's "succession" statutes. You may have definite ideas as to whom should inherit your estate. But, if there is no valid will in place at the time of your death, your estate will be divided according to that state's succession statutes.

*People called "snowbirds," or who split time between two states, must declare state of residency for taxes, driver's license, voting, etc.

Wills
A properly drafted *will* allows an individual to more effectively control the transfer of his/her property to the desired individuals or organizations specifically identified in the document.

Three specific requirements dictate what makes a will valid:
  (1) The creator must be at least eighteen years of age, and of sound mind;
  (2) The *will* should be prepared by a competent attorney, typewritten, and witnessed by two individuals;
  (3) However, a holographic *will* is acceptable (entirely written in the handwriting of the creator), signed and dated.

Advantages
You may designate beneficiaries and attach conditions to bequests. You may choose and appoint the *executor* or *guardian* of your estate to serve with or without a bond. You may also create a trust in the *will* for a spouse, minors, or other beneficiaries. These factors help to simplify the probate process—and a *will* may be revoked or amended at any time prior to death.

Disadvantages

Having a *will* does not avoid probate. It is only an instruction to the court as to how you wish your assets to be distributed. Another disadvantage is that there always exists a potential for a *will* to be contested by omitted heirs, or heirs who feel they should receive more than they did.

Probate

Probate is a court proceeding to supervise the orderly distribution of a decedent's property to his/her creditors, heirs, and beneficiaries. The assets not subject to probate are those held in joint tenancy, life insurance, pension plans and IRAs, or any assets held in trust.

Advantages

The greatest advantage of the probate process is that there is court supervision which provides better control of the distribution of the estate. There is also increased protection against theft or misuse of assets.

Disadvantages

A time-consuming process, which can cause prolonged delays in distribution of the estate's assets. It is also inconvenient and can be costly. Costs are regulated by statutes within the state of jurisdiction, and in most instances can be as high as five percent (5%) of the gross value of the estate, or greater.

Revocable Living Trust

A living trust is an arrangement whereby any chosen assets transferred to a trust are held, administered, and distributed by a trustee for the sole benefit of the named beneficiaries of the trust. The trustee must follow all of the terms and conditions imposed upon him/her by the creator of the trust. The creator of the trust can be both its trustee and beneficiary during his/her lifetime.

When a living trust is created, a Durable Power of Attorney for asset management and a Durable Power of Attorney for health care decisions in the event that the trustee cannot make such decisions, are typically created, also. There is also a directive to physicians and health care providers—also known as a "Living Will."

Advantages

One advantage to the Living Trust is there is no probate upon the death of the trustee or beneficiary of the trust. It is a private document that does not require public knowledge upon death, and provides protection in the event of incompetency. It is a flexible document that allows for further modifications or structuring. Another advantage is achieving a "stepped-up" basis for income tax purposes which can save a very large estate significant savings in federal taxation.

Disadvantages

The assets must be titled in the name of the trust, which requires changing real estate and personal property titles, stock accounts, and bank accounts. The initial cost to create a Living Trust is greater than the cost of creating only a *will*, therefore, a "Pour-over" Will is also needed. A Pour-over Will controls any assets not originally titled in the name of the trust—automatically adding any purchases made but not yet included when the creator dies; the Pour-over Will also appoints guardians for minor beneficiaries.

Irrevocable Life Insurance Trust

An irrevocable trust is an effective tool that allows life insurance proceeds to escape federal income and estate taxes upon the death of the insured. Life insurance owned within a revocable trust, or owned by an individual, is included in the overall estate value when computing federal estate taxes.

Existing life insurance policies may be transferred into the irrevocable trust; however, the insured must live for three years after the transfer to have the policy proceeds excluded from the estate. Any life insurance policies issued after the date of creation of the irrevocable trust do not have the three-year provision rules.

The premiums for the life insurance policy may be paid by gifting money into the irrevocable trust, which further removes asset value from the taxable estate.

The most common life insurance policy in an irrevocable trust is a second-to-die policy, which insures both the husband and wife within a marriage. The primary purpose is that the federal estate taxes are only due upon the second death of the married couple.

Additional Planning Techniques

Several other techniques may be employed to minimize the burden of federal and state taxation. A typical tool is the use of a "family limited partnership," which can be effective in legally receiving a reduction in the assets held within the *family limited partnership* due to the difficulty in liquidating an interest in an asset within a partnership.

Many families consider creating a "qualified personal residence trust" or "education trust" for children and grandchildren, or even a "generation-skipping trust."

Another method to reduce estate taxes is charitable giving. If there are no heirs, this is a desirable way to be certain that your estate goes to your favorite charity(ies) without taxation. If there are heirs, many purchase life insurance policies for the heirs as a means of wealth replacement, then leave the assets in the estate to charity. This technique ensures that heirs receive their inheritance without taxation, and favored charity(ies) receive a tax-free gift, as well. Numerous methods can be used to protect the estate that individuals work hard to amass. It is important to employ a qualified attorney and accountant to maximize estate-planning strategies.

The key to all of these tools is to begin the planning process as soon as possible—before unexpected or premature death occurs.

******

I close this book, a labor of love and memory, with words expressing my beliefs and feelings better than I could ever hope to write.

Gary R. Davis

A Psalm of Life

Lives of great men all remind us
We can make our lives sublime,
And, departing, leave behind us
Footprints on the sands of time;

Footprints, that perhaps another,
Sailing o'er life's solemn main,
A forlorn and shipwrecked brother,
Seeing, shall take heart again.

Let us, then, be up and doing,
With a heart for any fate;
Still achieving, still pursuing,
Learn to labor and to wait.
Henry Wadsworth Longfellow